To

Jo ann

THE AMERICAN DREAM

Enrica's Story

Daughter of Italian Immigrants in the South

Jo Ann Kersh

BRADHAM
PRESS

The American Dream
Enrica's Story
Daughter of Italian Immigrants in the South

by Jo Ann Kersh

Published by: Bradham Press
346 Sandy Cove
Clarksdale, MS 38614-2317
Telephone: (662) 902-3064
E-mail: BradhamPress@yahoo.com

ISBN: 978-0-9858386-0-7
Library of Congress Control Number: 2012943852

First Edition. Printed in the United States of America
10 9 8 7 6 5 4 3 2 1

Cover and Page Design by One-On-One Book Production, West Hills, California.

DEDICATION

To Mary, the Mother of God

To Vance, Reed and Wilkes

In Memory of Jimmie Moore Bradham

LA MADONNA DELLA ROSA

Venerate in Ostra (Diocesi di Senigallia)
incoronata il 1 Settembre 1726

ACKNOWLEDGMENTS

I am grateful to W.C., my husband for the past 11 years, for his encouragement in all of my endeavors. It was he who said, "just do it" when I struggled with trying to put Mama's journal into book form. He alone knows my emotional struggle.

To Will, my blue-eyed 'action' son, who made it happen by calling Alan Gadney with One-On-One Book Production and starting me on this adventure. He has told me that he thought that the American Dream was found in the pages of this book.

To my Celia who has remained silent most of the time, but guarded. She is so protective of me. How I wish I were more like her and less like myself.

To Alan Gadney and Carolyn Porter with One-On-One Book Production who have guided me, spoon fed me, throughout this process with kindness and a willingness to help me in all ways to reach this final place in the road.

My intent in writing this book is a singular one. I want to stand up and clap for all those people who struggled and survived, especially those who became role models in my life. My heartfelt thanks to every one of you.

And, to my grandsons, Vance, Reed and Wilkes, who can learn much from reading this book. These people, our people, were the stepping stones to a better life for us all. Especially for you. You are my heart.

CONTENTS

PREFACE

It is a joy to share with you Mama's journal – the true story of a young lady born in the early 1900s to Italian immigrants in the Mississippi Delta and how they lovingly survived. They worked hard and played hard (her words) and ultimately lived the American Dream.

Of course, events happen in life that can change everything. In 1943, Mama, Enrica, found herself straddled with four kids, no money and little education. She drew on deep inner strength and faith to survive. Along the way, she forgave and accepted the hand dealt her, circled us with love and affection and always, always was there for us through it all.

We were twice blessed because she lived long enough for us to tell her how much she meant to all of us. It is my hope that you will learn to love her too through these pages.

INTRODUCTION

For where your treasure is,
there also will your heart be.
Luke 12: 34.

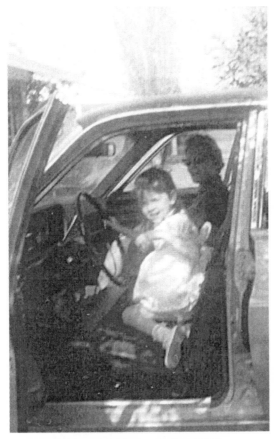

Celia with Mama in the MGB.

Enrica Antici Furini died on March 18, 2002, at 1 a.m., just five days shy of her 88th birthday. She was as alone as if she had died on that cold bathroom floor weeks earlier, but then, she had lived alone for almost 40 years. The stroke that knocked her to the ground and wedged her body between the bathtub and commode happened during the night. That is where we found her, helpless, on the floor. Totally paralyzed on one side, she lived the next six weeks in the extended care wing of the local hospital. At nine sharp the staff shut and locked those vault-like doors and family members had to leave. After her death we were invited into the room to see her – one more time. Her body was still warm. Her presence was still felt. We would later hear from Michael Jacob, Eucharistic Minister for St. Elizabeth's Church, that he had prayed with her in the late evening and that Mama raised her hand to make the Sign of the Cross with him. She was a strong Catholic. He said his knees buckled when he realized she was fully aware of his presence.

After a while, we gathered her meager possessions from the hospital room, and we all agreed to meet later, to make arrangements for the funeral Mass. There were no surprises. She had prepaid the funeral expenses. Burial plots had been purchased years earlier, and she had paid for the monument and given a few instructions including her desire for the coffin to be closed.

We four children and our spouses went to her home. As we pulled into her driveway, the reality of her death hit us hard – it was as though we were almost smothering. I, for one, could not bear seeing that old antique avocado green Ford Falcon under the car-port – without her. We had laughed about it forever. A bomb – it really was. The grandchildren had named it MGB (Mamaw's green bug). But, she loved that car like you would love a best friend.

Final clothes needed to be picked out. And we de-cided to bury her with the rosary made especially for her as a gift many years earlier. Mary Ann, one of my sisters, designed the rosary with each bead represent-ing a family member. My bead was green – for emer-ald – representing May, my birth month. I remember one bead was extra and Mary Ann put a crystal bead there – for children born after the rosary was complet-ed. Mama treasured that rosary, and it seemed fitting to let it rest with her.

It might have been that day or a few days later that we began going through her material possessions. There were so few. She had so little. Mildred and Mary Ann found the journal and Mary Ann read it first. It was a fascinating read – an interesting factual account-ing of Mama's life here in the Mississippi Delta at the turn of the century and later, with the last entry being a statement about daddy leaving her in December 1943.

Mama and her beloved "MGB"

THE JOURNAL

Give thanks to the Lord for he is good,
for his kindness endures forever.
1 Chronicles 16:34.

Picture of the enclosed well at the
Madonna della Rosa church in Ostra, Italy.

The Antici Family celebrating First Communion or Confirmation for the two older children. Mama is third child from left.

IN MEMORY OF GRANDMOTHER MARIA PIRANI ANTICI

1891 – 1981

It's spring in my little town, population 18,000. Traveling to Clarksdale, or leaving from here, all roads take you through miles and miles of farmland – so barren during the winter you can see for miles in any direction – now busy with tractors stirring up the rich Delta soil, readying the land for planting. Already, many acres are polka dotted with pale green seedlings, and in a few weeks I will be able to distinguish between cotton plants and soy bean plants. Wheat, corn and peanuts will soon be taking their places in the Delta scenery, so close to the mighty Mississippi you can almost shake your fist at it.

It was in between the cotton rows and the shacks that the Blues began in Mississippi, and it was in between these rows and shacks that my mother and her parents toiled in this part of the world where each spring brings new beginnings.

My grandmother, Maria, was a live-in servant at the age of 12, an indentured servant at 14, became wife to my grandfather at the age of 18 and bore him nine children. Bowed from bending over the hoe, the scrub board, the cutting board, the iron, the sewing machine, she had to lift her head to look at you

3

with those blue-green eyes, that wiry grey hair circling her face in glory. She knew well the labor of the land, and she knew well – peace within.

1

BEGINNING

The journal, 87 handwritten pages, begins with Mama's birth and then jumps backward and forward in time as she remembered happenings in the family and jotted down her thoughts. Most of the journal is written in present tense as if she is reliving everything she is writing. It oozes with love and respect for family. Mama often said, "they worked hard and played hard" and those of us who read the journal found that to be true. They prayed hard too. It was not an easy read, however, well worth it.

The journal is about her family. That was its purpose: Mama telling us about the lives of her parents, immigrants from Italy to America and the hot humid Mississippi Delta and the nine children born to this union, Enrica, (Mama) being the fourth. Son, Edwino, and two daughters, Isolina and Editha, were the oldest and the last five children according to age were Elena, Marino, Angelina, Theresa and Antonio. Grandma and Grandpa gave their children Italian names, but they were Americanized to Lizzie, Frank (somehow Edwino became Frank), Edith, Riga, Lena, Mike, Angie, Theresa and Tony. They lived in America; their children were American. Outside the home, Filippo Antici became Phillip Antici and Maria Pirani Antici became Mary Antici.

My grandfather, Filippo – lovingly called PePo by many – was born in Ostra, Italy, on September 13, 1880. He was one of four children born to Antonio Antici and Teresa Pacenti Antici. His siblings were named Chester, Palmina and Vincent, but Mama had no further information on them. However, she was able to visit their graves in 1987.

Phillip Antici home in Ostra, Italy

Grandpa decided when he was a young single man to come to America as an indentured farm laborer along with two or three other families. In the fall of 1904, he sailed from Genoa, Italy. He was 24 years old. He was indentured by Jake Aldridge who was a farmer in Arcola, Mississippi. He paid the boat fare to Ellis Island, New York, and also the train ride to the Delta. Care packages were provided for the workers to eat on the train as they traveled to the plantations. Grandpa was committed to be an indebted worker to Mr. Aldridge for two years.

A funny side note – bologna was in every care package. Those poor Italian foreigners had never heard of bologna and were told it was made from horse meat so they wouldn't eat it. We laughed about this because over time Grandpa liked bologna as we all did.

Grandpa never talked about his trip except that it took 22 days on the ocean, then another three days by train to arrive in Arcola. He was looking for a better life and gambled on finding it here in America. Mama said he worked long hard hours for very little money, but when the debt was paid, he was free.

After becoming independent, Grandpa worked as a day laborer. He, once, told me a story about those days. He was supposed to get to the field before sunup in order to be ready to begin work at first light. One morning he got to the field just as the sun was rising and his employer, pointing to the east, said, "Filippo, you see the sun?" Grandpa acknowledged that he did. His employer then announced, "You don't get paid today." Grandpa hit his fist on his leg in anger when remembering this event. He told me he was never late after that. It was a tough lesson – he never forgot.

Rizzieri Furini, the man who would later be my grandfather on my father's side, had an unfortunate experience when he came to this country. He apparently had a misunderstanding about how long he had to work for the farmer who paid his boat fare and he left the farm. The farmer searched and found him and made him return to the farm making it clear how long Furini was to work there. Mostly, these laborers could not read or write.

Grandma's Family

1919 photo of Guadinzo and Anna Pirani, Grandma's parents. Grandma and two of her sisters were married and not in the picture.

On December 13, 1905, Guadinzo Pirani and his wife, Anna Filouri Pirani, and their eight children set sail from Genoa and in 21 days arrived at Ellis Island. Mama mentioned that Guadinzo was an orphan and had two or three brothers, but he did not stay in touch with them. The Pirani's also rode the train to Arcola to work for another farmer named Andrew Aldridge, and it took them three years to pay off their debt. In 1905, Grandma, Maria Pirani, was 14 years old. She had an older sister, actually half sister, Santa, and six other siblings.

Some might say that the Aldridge farmers paid for the trips to this country because they needed cheap labor, but what a golden opportunity they offered to the families who accepted their offers. The immigrants came seeking a better life, and it was found here in the cotton fields, working from sun up to sun down, hard physical labor, living in shacks, depending on the fairness of their bosses. They rarely spoke of those first years; they were just a part of the process of entering into a new life.

My grandparents were born and lived their young lives in Ostra, Italy. They both attended Mass at the Madonna della Rosa Church in Ostra, but they did not meet there. They met in America – on a farm – in Washington County – in the State of Mississippi.

When my grandparents left Italy the Madonna della Rosa Church was much smaller than it is today. There was a well outside the main church which could be used by the towns people. During World War II, the area was destroyed, and the people were left without any water except for the well at the church which became their only source of water. Father Natale Boindini, a family friend who lived in Ostra, said that the water in the well never got lower or higher during that critical time. Later, after the war, the well was incorporated into the main church, and the water continues to be the same level all the time.

When the day came when Grandpa decided he wanted to be married, he went to Great Grandpa Pirani and asked him for one of his daughters to be his wife. Great Grandpa told him to come back the next year, and he did. He married Grandma on January 24, 1909.

He told a funny story about himself and Grandma. He said he gave her $50 before they were married to let her know his good intentions and, when they were married, he took the money back because she now belonged to him and so did the money. True or not true, Grandpa loved his Maria. He sang her name, Ma-Ri'-A. Often, he said he wished he had not waited so long to get married. Grandma was the first to call him her pet name "PePo." It is amazing to me how much they loved each other. Working side by side everyday, eking out a living from the soil, depending upon each other for everything, and praying together made for a good solid marriage. Neither of them had any schooling. Grandma could read a little printed Italian. It was enough for her to read her prayer book. Mama said that the only book in the house was Grandma's prayer book except for school books when they went to school. Grandpa couldn't read or write. Mama described both of them as hard working people. Even though you might think Grandpa was handicapped, he wasn't. He could add a column of figures before you got out your pen and paper. He could look at something and build what he needed. And he never missed an opportunity to pick up a discarded scrap for future use. Mama said you couldn't beat him out of a penny. Phillip and Mary were a team, a good team.

When they got married, Grandpa was farming 10 or 12 acres of land in Arcola in Washington County, Mississippi. A year later, on February 20, 1910, their first child, Lizzie, was born.

Sixteen months later, on June 28, 1911, Frank was born. Later that year the family of four sailed to Italy to help Grandpa's father pay out some old debt, and they remained there until the fall of 1912. Sadly, there was friction. I never knew the whole story, but Grandpa left angry at one of his brothers and with his father begging him not to leave. They never went back. Edith, conceived in Italy, was born on February 11, 1913, and our Mama followed on March 13, 1914. She wrote in her journal that Grandpa wanted a boy. Her words, "All he got was a male voice, strength and courage. The rest was all female." Mama called herself a "rough and tough tom girl."

I have to laugh. Mama's voice was deep. People always said "yes, sir" and "no, sir" to her over the phone.

On March 29, 1914, Mama was baptized "Enrica" by Father P. Gabrielli, a Catholic priest. She said that Grandma did not come for the baptism as she was not allowed to enter the church without a special blessing. It was also their custom to rest for 30 or 40 days after delivery. We think Mama was probably named after St. Rita of Cascia, Italy. Grandma knew her saints and St. Rita could have been a favorite.

In those days, priests mostly said Mass in homes because there were no church buildings. If a family had a big house, the Mass would be said once a month, sometimes every other month. The poor immigrants kept their faith alive by praying the rosary and litany to the Blessed Virgin Mary every night. They also included prayers to lots of saints. Mama remembered that sometimes Grandpa would say, "Maria, how many more saints are you going to add?" He had more chores; she had more prayers.

They said morning prayers and night prayers. Mama learned to pray in Italian and continued praying that way all of her life.

"The fall of 1914 the family moved to Duncan, Bolivar County, Mississippi, and on June 4, 1915, Lena was born."

Mike was born on December 13, 1916. Mama recalled vividly the night he was born. It is amazing because she wasn't quite three years old at the time. She remembered that the children were all sitting on the floor in front of the fireplace for heat and for light because all the lamps were in the bedroom with Grandma and some midwives who were helping with the delivery. Lizzie was holding Lena in her arms, and Frank, Edith and Mama were huddled together. She remembered that it was cold and wet outside. One of the midwives' husband, a Mr. Alvatroni, told the children he found a baby boy in a wagon track and about that time the baby started crying. Mama said they believed him. Later in her journal she said that midwives delivered all of their children.

Her memory was sharp. She tells us in the journal what life was really like for the family. Grandma worked the fields alongside Grandpa. When she went to the field, she locked the door to the house – leaving baby Mike inside. She left the three sisters, Edith, age four,

Lena, age two, and Mama, age three, on the porch with a bucket of water. The two older children, Frank and Lizzie, were helping in the field. When the baby cried, one of the three sisters would run to the field and call Grandma. She would come home and feed baby Mike and attend to his needs. Grandma also set the clock so that when the alarm went off, one of the children went to the field to ask her to come home and prepare dinner. Mama said, "This went on with all of the babies."

The children began working in the fields when they were six or seven years old with the youngest keeping watch at home. They all had to work hard to "keep things going on." At six years of age they were picking cotton. At eight, they were chopping cotton and corn, clearing out the weeds. They had to learn what was cotton and what was a weed.

Mama recalled that the younger children would skip and hop all the way home. They made a game out of work. She said that they were all happy, and the Lord blessed them with good health. Truth is they didn't know what a doctor was, and of course, had never heard of a drug store or medicine. She explains later in the journal how Grandma attended to their hurts. Everything she did worked.

The children did not always have shoes. During the summer the ground was hot; if they stepped on a rock or nail it felt like "a coal of fire." She said the bottoms of their feet were like leather.

Three more children were born to the family. Angie was born on November 18, 1918. The family had moved to Shaw, Mississippi, the previous fall. Grandpa was always looking for more land, better land, more opportunities to feed his family.

Two or three pages of the journal were devoted to describing a storm that caused a lot of trouble for the family. Again, her memory was vivid.

On a seemingly quiet Sunday evening after dinner, Lizzie was helping Grandma with the dishes. They never really threw anything away so the scraps were put into a dish for the dogs. When Lizzie stepped out on the porch with the scraps she noticed a storm coming. They all saw the rolling clouds and the lightening and heard the thunder. Suddenly, a lightening bolt hit the kitchen chimney. It came down the chimney in the stovepipe, and circled around the stove. Then, it went through the floor into the ground. There was a hole in the floor where it exited and smoke was everywhere.

The children screamed. Lizzie said she felt like someone hit her in the stomach. Edith had been combing Angie's hair in the bedroom when some object hit her ear. She grabbed the little one and ran into the front room with the rest of the family. The red mark on her ear terrified the children even more. Soot covered everybody and everything. Grandpa threw open the kitchen door to let the smoke out and to let fresh air in.

When the storm was over they went outside to assess the damages. The top part of the chimney that rises above the roof was gone. Bricks were everywhere. Under the house a No. 3 (3 representing 30 gallon) aluminum tub was one-third full of dirt. Grandma and Grandpa sent all the children except Frank to a neighbor's house while they cleaned up the mess. Later, Mrs.

Gussoni gave the children a loaf of knot bread, and they rushed home with their treasure.

Grandma's little black leather prayer book was well worn when she died. I imagine this was one of those times when she picked it up and prayed.

Mama said the storm, the lightening striking the house, taught all of them a lesson. "Don't stay outside if a storm is close by." She talked about all she saw in this storm and in others. She saw lightening hitting trees and splitting them in half. On some trees the bark was pulled off. When lightening hit in an open field, it made a circle ten feet wide. It would kill cotton and grass within the circle. When lightening fell to the ground the children closed their ears. They found arrows in the circles caused by lightening and called them "lightening." She said some called them "Indian arrows." "They were pretty. The edges were real sharp. They had a sharp point. The top was shaped like a heart with a stem in the middle. It was about three inches long and two and three/fourth inches wide. The arrow was one/fourth to one/half inch thick. It had some shiny spots and some rough spots. It was pretty. It was not brick or iron. They were hard to break. Some of the arrows were big."

Mama was absolutely in awe of the lightening and the arrows.

In the fall of 1919, the family moved to Mattson, Mississippi. Grandpa again was looking for a better deal. Their sixth daughter, Theresa, was born on November 26, 1920. Mama said she was named after Grandpa's mother, but the names were spelled differently.

That same fall Grandma's parents, the Piranis,

with two single daughters and two single sons, moved to Fresno, California. Their son Ned and wife Ester moved as well. Also moving was their daughter Rosa and her husband Ned and their four children. Later, in 1927, Santa and her family moved. There is no explanation as to why they moved and why Grandma and Grandpa did not.

Grandma and Grandpa visiting relatives in Fresno, California

In 1922, the Antici family and their eight children moved to Coahoma County, Mississippi, on the Sommers place. By then Grandpa was working more land. He had the children help chop cotton and pick cotton and help with all the chores involving mules, hogs, chickens and a garden.

They moved a lot, and while Mama described every house, they all seemed the same. They were all "L" shaped – three bedrooms and a sitting room/kitchen. The porch was the length of three of the rooms. The five older girls slept in one bedroom, two on one bed

and three on the other. Two boys slept in another bedroom, and Grandma and Grandpa had the baby with
them in the third bedroom. They had an eating room
that was also used for a sitting room when they were
not working. Mama described that room as a room
with a big table and hard wood chairs, a sewing machine and a little stool with a bucket of water and a
dipper. The stool was in the corner near the front door
so the children could drink when they went out and
when they came into the house.

Because the church rule was no food or drink after midnight, Mama made a mistake on her First Holy
Communion Day. She got a drink of water as they
were leaving the house. Grandma told the priest how
sorry she was, and he let her receive Communion.

The outhouses were always set away from the house,
way behind the barn so people could not see them from
the house or smell the odor. "In cold weather we put
on our coats and ran to the toilet. On the way back
to the house, we stopped on the porch where Mama
(Grandma) would have some hot water and one bucket
of cold water. We put the mixed water in the face pan
and washed our faces. We had a homemade towel hanging on a nail. We dried our faces and then ran into the
house. Sometimes the water would freeze, and we had
to break the ice to wash our faces. It was cold."

Mama said they only used pee pots at night, or if,
they had a storm in the daytime. If they had a light rain
and needed to use the toilet, they ran to the outhouse
and back. If rain was pouring down hard, they stopped
at the shed and waited. If it began really storming they
ran all the way.

In speaking of the houses they lived in, Mama referred to them as old shacks with cracks in the walls. She remembered seeing snow come in the houses through the cracks. She went on to describe them further. There was no paint outside, no paper inside, no cabinets in the kitchen, and no counter tops. There was a pantry that had shelves for dishes. There was no heat in the bedrooms so, Lizzie would heat an iron-like brick called a warmer and run it under the covers before the younger ones went to bed. Mama mentioned waking up in the winter with ice on the sheets where they had been breathing.

Mama was a dreamer and a sleepwalker. One night she dreamed she was in the barn where the cotton was kept. She wanted to hide her cotton sack from somebody in the dream. She pulled the sheet off the bed and put it behind the bedroom door. In the morning Grandma asked who put the sheet on the floor. She told her she was hiding her cotton sack, and they all had a good laugh.

It was in 1918 or 1919 that Grandpa bought his first car – an Ovalen.

Mama tells of a big event that happened on September 13, 1923, Grandpa's birthday. Celebrating his own birthday, Grandpa came home from town with five gallons of ice cream. "We had to ask all our neighbors to come and help eat the ice cream. This was the first time we had ice cream. The crops had to look good for him to do that. We all had a big time."

The next year, almost on Grandpa's birthday, Tony, named after Grandpa's father, was born. The date was September 5, 1924. He was the ninth and last child born to Phillip and Mary Antici.

In the fall of 1925, the family moved again to a Mr. Tony's place in Coahoma County. It was south of Clarksdale. Mama once again described an "L" shaped house with the only difference being that the girls, all six of them, now slept in one bedroom, three in each bed.

Summer of 1947 Mama visited Grandma's sisters, brothers and their families in Fresno. Mama is standing second from right.

Grandma's youngest brother, August and his wife, Annette, two of our favorite California relatives.

IN MEMORY OF GODMOTHER
LENA ANTICI GRATTAFIORI
1915 – 1993

Earlier today it looked like somebody had pushed the sun into a fluffy down of clouds, making the sky hazy. Nothing like the morning I witnessed the phenomena that reminded me of my Godmother, Lena.

At 4 a.m. everything is supposed to be dark, so when I exited the bedroom with robe in hand, I was startled to see the brightness in the front foyer. I overslept, I thought, as I rushed into the den and opened the shutters and threw up the sash and saw that it truly was daylight, but, more than that. Stepping outside and looking to the east I saw what I find difficult to describe, a sky with no boundaries in red, orange, gold, fused together, the source of the brilliance I had noticed. Looking in the other direction, the shed, painted white, was showing off in colors and behind it, slightly to the right of it, was a rainbow. No regular rainbow, no McDonald's bow, much higher, more awesome. It reached midway into the sky and I knew I had to see its ending. Again, rushing through the kitchen, I looked at the clock with numbers two inches long and see that it registers 4:11. At the end of the garage, I didn't have to look far. To the left of the house is the end of that magnificent rainbow. I kept saying to myself that this isn't possible; I knew it was four o'clock. Then, suddenly the rainbow disappeared, it was dark and I re-entered the house, closed the blinds, got a cup of coffee and wondered at the marvels of our Creator.

It wasn't her gardening, though her yard was a showplace, and it wasn't her working abilities, she never worked outside the home, that endeared me to Aunt Lena. She never did an extraordinary thing, yet she lived an extraordinary life – in pure simplicity.

She married, became a homemaker, tended to the yard, the garden, the house. A mother to one child, she lost her second child, stillborn. Lunch was served every day in the dining room, in full view of the statues and flowers she had placed on the mantel, a makeshift altar. She tricked me once, serving me a slice of fried eggplant and telling me it was steak.

When you live close to the land, when you are in close communion with the simple beauty of your surroundings, your life just blossoms. It becomes a shining star, a rainbow of hope. Such was her life – my godmother, my friend.

2
WORKING AND GARDENING

The children all had responsibilities. "Every morning of the year, even on Christmas, Easter, or some big Holy Day, Edith, Lena and I would take the pee pots out, empty them and go to the pump and rinse them. In the wintertime, we would run but in the summertime, we would take our time – and talk."

The girls had to clean the lamp globes, trim the wicks, and put kerosene in the lamps. They only had three lamps, one in the kitchen, one in the front room and one in Grandma's bedroom. Grandma's lamp was kept on all night because of small children. Also, so everyone could see a bucket of water and a dipper that she kept by the door.

Grandma was smart. She probably slept with one eye open. If any of the children ate too much of her good ham, she would catch the thief by seeing who drank a lot of water during the night. Mama confessed that when she got her fill of ham she was thirsty but would not get up to drink.

She was very sneaky. She loved Italian cheese and would cut a slice for herself and run outside to eat it. Grandma said whoever ate too much cheese would lose their teeth. I think Mama had all of her teeth when she died.

They had other jobs as well. They had to pump water for the mules, and fill the drinking trough, which took over an hour. The four mules, Tom, Bob, Nellie and Fannie would quickly empty the trough and then they would have to pump more water for them. Mama said, "That used to make me so mad." She must have been quite young because she said that Grandpa put a long handle over the short pump handle so the smaller children could pull on the handle. Mama said she would chase the mules away. But they would kick their heels, blow out a train of smoke and come back and drink again. That is the only chore she really complained about.

It was at the house on Mr. Tony's place that Grandpa drilled for water.

"Next to the steps, Papa drove the iron pipe down in the ground. I don't remember how many feet deep. This was for the pump. We watched them drive those pipes in the ground. We would cover our ears. Papa put the pump on the iron pipe, primed the pump and up came the water. If the water did not look good, they would drive another pipe down.

"The water had lots of iron in it, but we used it to cook with and to wash clothes. Sometimes, if we wanted some cold water, we would pump for a little while longer. Then cold water came up and we would drink it, but Papa thought it best to haul water from town for us to drink."

They fed the hogs, fed and milked the cows. They had to husk the corn. They would also put the cob in a grinder to shell it for feeding the chickens and hogs. Sometimes the cows and mules got corn too. Sometimes the hogs got corn on the cob. They also had to cut sugar cane to feed the animals.

"In the springtime, when we chopped cotton, we went out real early. We would sit on the road waiting for the sun to come up. We chopped for about two hours before we ate breakfast." Grandma would put a big dish towel over the screen door to let the children know breakfast was ready. It quite often was homemade bread cut in bite-sized pieces and placed in a big dish. Grandma warmed milk and made coffee, adding just enough to give the milk a little color. (That is how Mama served coffee to us.) The children ate all they wanted. "There was always enough for everybody. We would wash our hands, eat breakfast, run to the outhouse, wash our hands, and then head back to the field."

As the children grew older they needed more food. Mama told how Grandma cooked eggs with the leaves from the garlic plant. She chopped the leaves real fine, mixed them in with the eggs, added parmesan cheese and scrambled them for their breakfast. Sometimes they had sausage, salami or ham, all home cured, with a fried egg and bread for breakfast. They always had enough.

"When the towel went up again, we would go home for lunch. We washed our hands, ate lunch and helped with the dishes. We had one hour to rest or play. Then, we went back into the field until dark. This went on every year."

"In the spring we chopped cotton, then we harvested the hay and corn, and in the fall we picked cotton."

During lay-by time (when the chopping had been done and the farmers were waiting for the bolls to open), Grandpa, Frank and Mike, when he got old enough, would go to the woods in early morning and cut trees. They sawed the logs 26 to 28 inches long for the fireplace and 10 inches long for the stove. They split the logs, loaded the wagon, and when they got home, they stacked the wood in a long pile.

In the wintertime, in addition to their other chores, they had to bring in wood for the fireplace. Originally, all the cooking was done in the fireplace and required big pieces of wood but Grandpa bought a wood burning stove in the mid- 1920s so they did not have to feed the fireplace in summer.

Earlier, Mama talked about their early morning jobs. Now she devotes many pages to their day jobs and evening jobs. "As we got older our jobs got harder. We worked in the garden, pulling the suckers from the tomato plants, tying the tomatoes up, chopping the garden soil and pulling all the weeds up. We cut the lettuce and cleaned and washed it. We had chickory, endive, head lettuce and lettuce that grew tall the shape of a comb. It was 10 to 12 inches high. We all loved to eat the core. It was about seven-or eight-inches long. We pulled the leaves off, cleaned the lettuce and saved the core. The one who cleaned the lettuce ate the core."

Once again, the details are there.

"When the tomatoes, eggplants, peppers, butter beans, sweet peas were ready, we had to pick them and wash them to get ready for canning. Next came beets, carrots, squash, zucchini, cabbage, swiss chard, turnip and mustard greens, ceci beans and fava (horse beans)." They also grew spinach, snap beans and collard greens, artichokes, celery, parsley, fennel, mint, sweet basil and rosemary, Irish potatoes and sweet potatoes.

Grandpa built a little storage hut with bricks, mud and straw. He lined the inside with hay and put the sweet potatoes in there for the winter. He made a door about 18 inches high and 12 inches wide. Details, details. They opened the doors and reached inside for the potatoes. "I never did think about a snake. I shiver now when I think about that. We lived way out in the country. God was with us."

The vegetables kept them busy all summer. They would go out in the field and pick the corn before it got too hard to eat. They had to water the garden every day when it did not rain, using one bucket or two buckets at a time. It was hard work and it was hot. As usual, they had no shoes on their feet.

They gathered eggs daily – 20 to 25 in summer and 10 to 15 in the winter.

They also raised peanuts. "In the late summer we would pull the peanuts up and spread them out for the sun to dry. We would wash them after they were dried and put them in big bags. Later we would roast them after the bread was baked."

When they were young, they did not work in the field on Holy Days. They went to Mass and stayed home. "Many years later we would go to Mass first and then go to the field. All the other farmers were in the field. They did not go to Mass. The grass would be taking the cotton over so we had to chop it down. Papa asked the priest if it was wrong to work in the field on Holy Days. The priest told him we could work in the field because the money from the cotton was our living."

In July, just before lay-by time, they would go all over the field and cut down all the tall weeds. The weeds were taller than the cotton. "All you could see was our straw hats."

"When that was done, we went to the hay. We helped load the wagon with the big hayfork. Let me tell you, it was hard work. And hot. Some of the hay would get down our backs. Sometimes there was a snake under those little piles of hay. One time it was a blue runner. It was running with the head about one foot from the ground. Dan Jose, a friend and neighbor, chased it and killed it with the hayfork. It scared the mules. We had to grab the rope and hold them.

"One time, when I was 14 years old, something scared the mules and they started to run with Papa in the wagon. Papa could not reach the rope. The mules were running wild over cotton rows and over a ditch. We all were yelling 'Stop, Tom. Stop, Fannie.' But they kept running. We were crying, afraid Papa would get hurt or he would be killed. They ran about one and a half miles before one of our neighbors saw the runaway mules. He got on his mule, went in front of the wagon, grabbed the lines and stopped the mules. By that time, Papa was lying down on the hay, and he was holding on to the hayfork, hanging on for dear life. All we could do was watch those crazy mules run. When Papa came back to the field, we finished loading the wagon. That was one time I was glad I wasn't on top of that wagon. Thank you, God. Thanks again, Papa was safe.

"We went home, unloaded the wagon, and Papa got Tom first. Let me tell you, he whipped that mule. He went inside of the fence so Tom could not run away. Then he got Fannie and he let her have it. We stood right there and watched Papa whip those mules. They kicked and talked back to him, but Papa had control of them. We were glad Papa whipped them. We loved Papa."

As each load of hay was brought home, they built a haystack. Some of the children would help pack the hay while others would get the hay and pile it on the haystack. When the stack got to be five-feet high, the younger ones would get off, and the older ones would keep on helping pack the hay. Then the neighbors would take over. "We kept busy raking the hay around the stack and playing water girl. When the stack got 20 -or 30 -feet tall, just one person could stay up there. When he finished the stack, they put up a ladder 13 -to 14 -feet long so he could climb down. Those haystacks were good to look at. They were packed so hard that rain could not get in a stack."

Later, there would be no need for the haystack. Instead, the hay was baled using a machine pulled by one mule. Someone had to lead the mule in a circle, going round and round. Another person would feed the hay into the machine. It would come out in a bale with wire around it. Then, the hay was stored for feed for the mules during the winter. During the summer the mules ate sorghum sugar cane and corn.

"After the hay was in, we started on the corn. The younger ones would go in front of the mules and wagon, pick the corn off the stalk on the row that the wagon would go over, and make little piles of corn on the next row. We would snap the ears of corn from the stalk and throw them into the wagon. We really had to work fast to keep up with the wagon. Sometimes we had to stop the mules so we could catch up and pick up the piles of corn on the ground dropped there by those who were picking the corn from the middle row. It was hard work and as usual it was very hot work. (It is hard to understand, but I think they picked three rows at a time. Children in the middle row walked in front of the wagon and picked corn and threw it in rows one and three. The wagon was in the center row. Picking three rows at a time, it must have taken days to complete the job.) We were out in 100 degrees weather. I don't know how many times we went up and down those rows. We had four or five acres of corn.

"We had to get the husk off the ear of corn and let the corn dry. We used to shell the corn by hand until Papa bought a corn grinder. It was still hard, but much better and faster. We took turns. We knew when our turn came around. We didn't forget because Mama would get on us."

The family had a number of farm animals. They had four mules, two cows, one calf and three or four hogs. They raised chickens, turkeys, guinea hens, ducks and pigeons. Grandpa built a big pigeon house, five-by-five-feet, three stories high. They used pigeons for spaghetti sauce or baked them with potatoes. They also had 30 to 40 tame rabbits and a dog and a cat.

"When all our summer work was finished we started picking cotton. Just us children would pick one bale of cotton by the 13th of September, Papa's birthday. Papa was not a good cotton picker." He would hold the boll with one hand and pick one lock at a time. They had to tell him how to pick cotton. "He never could get all the locks out at one time, but he tried. Mama (Grandma) used to do all the picking with very little help from Papa. He was slow."

In the fall, Grandpa would get the children up very early in the morning. He would call their names and tell them he had a little whiskey for them. He wanted to help them wake up. They didn't want to drink the whiskey because it burned their stomachs.

"One day during picking season, I was cutting some ham for my younger sisters and brother. I was holding the big piece of ham in my hand. When I cut the piece for me, I cut a big piece and cut my finger. It was a bad cut. That mark will go to the grave with me. We washed it with kerosene and put sugar on it to stop the bleeding. I kept it wrapped up with a piece of rag so that I could pick cotton. Papa got on me one day because Lena picked more cotton than me. About two weeks after I cut my finger with the knife, I burst it open with the axe. I was trying to cut the buckle off a belt. I was in trouble. There was infection and more washing with kerosene and sugar. I still picked cotton. Sometimes I cried to myself because the finger was hurting so bad. The top of the cotton boll would hit the end of my finger. Lena only picked more than me one day.

"By the end of September we had black people from town to help pick the cotton. Papa would drive to town and pick them up."

When he was picking up choppers or pickers he would drive to town in his 1926 or 1927 Buick. When he turned it on, the car would make a lot of noise. He would drive around the house twice before taking off for town to pick up the workers. It would be around 4:30 or 5:00 in the morning. Mama said Grandpa would rev up the engine to be sure we all were up and ready to work when he got home.

"We would have 15 to 20 black folks picking cotton. Out of the 20, one man picked more than me. I picked 306 pounds. The man had 319 pounds. That was my first and last time for 306 pounds. But I picked over 200 pounds quite a few times. I forget what Papa gave me for picking 306 pounds. Whatever it was, I was happy. It could have been five to 25 cents. I was glad. We did not see money too often when we were below our teens." She asked, "Can you imagine picking cotton in 100 degrees weather? You would not have a dry thread on your clothes. But we lived through it all. Hot or cold, we were out in it.

"Papa would come out in the field with some wine and bread and a bowl. He poured wine in the bowl for us to dip our bread. Papa was a kind hearted person.

He felt sorry for us, but he knew we had to work to survive. He would do that at 10 o'clock in the morning. The bread and wine were good. We were happy to get it, and we got to rest for 20 to 30 minutes. In the fall, Mama would send Tony with baked sweet potatoes for us to eat around 3:30 in the afternoon. We were always glad to get some food. When Tony was old enough to work in the field, Papa would bring the potatoes. This went on year after year."

Mama does say that the three younger children did not have to work hard like they did. "Things had changed a lot as they grew up."

Edith was a clown, the clown of the family. Mama told us a story about her in the cotton field. They had been to Mass on Sunday, and the gospel was about Jesus saying "a little while and you will not see me, and again in a little while you will see me." Edith stood up in the cotton field and said, "in a little while you shall see me" and then ducked down and said, "in a little while you will not see me." She said they threw cotton bolls at her, and she would run and do it all over again.

More work. "We pumped water for two big barrels." (The barrels used for water were not the same barrels Grandpa used for making wine). Grandma or Grandpa would slack the water with lime so it could be used for cooking and for laundry. It made the water real soft. They always put a washtub next to the house so when it rained the rain water would fill the tub. They poured the water out slowly because it had a lot of grime in the bottom. With this water, they shampooed their hair, using Grandma's homemade soap.

"We washed our hair outside in the summer and in the kitchen in the winter. Three or four of us shampooed at a time. We would have fun. This went on every year as long as we were single."

In addition to everything else, Mama says, "We made our butter. Mama (Grandma) would let the milk sour over night, put it in a two-gallon crock pot. The pot was 15-inches tall. The lid had a hole in the center. We had a handle with a paddle on one end. We put the handle through the hole. We would work the handle up and down. We churned and churned. We had our feet around the crock pot. I would get so tired sitting on the porch working that handle up and down, for a while with my right hand, then my left. I would pull the handle up over the hole to check for butter crumbs. When the crumbs showed up, I would work faster. When it was ready, with a strainer, we would get all the butter out and put it in a bowl. We put a dinner plate over the bowl and pressed all the milk out. That was good butter. We sold the buttermilk to both white and black people. What we did not sell, we fed the hogs. This went on every year. We did this when we were eight or nine years old. It can wear you out."

"In the summertime, Mama would hang a bucket full of milk outside on a hook from the porch ceiling. One night a bat fell in the bucket. It was the first time I saw what a bat looked like, with arms and legs connected by membranes which are used as wings. The body looked like a mouse, with wings. Well, the pigs got the milk. Lena and I were glad we did not have to churn that day.

"We were a hard working, happy family. We didn't get paid with money for the work we did. Room and board was our pay. The only time Papa paid us was when we picked cotton on Saturday afternoons. We got two or three cents a pound. Some made 30 cents, some 40 cents, and some got 50 cents. We only picked for three or four hours."

They all had to take a bath and wash the clothes. On Sunday, after Mass, Grandpa would stop at Mr. Albino's store, and the children would spend the money they had made. She says, "some of the candies were one cent, gum was five cents."

IN MEMORY
OF MIKE ANTICI

1916 – 1990

Uncle Mike was a lightweight boxer, an inventor of more than one patented product, he became nurse to his wife, the mother of his six children, who had an incurable lung disease – it took her breath away – by the second, for years, until it finally let her go.

He had run the FMH Grocery Store on Fourth Street for a while, became a farmer, and it was in that arena that he became an inventor. He wasn't the sort of person you would imagine sitting patiently with an ailing wife, crocheting afghans. He did though, devoted the years to her. He cooked, he cleaned, attended to all of their affairs.

When she died he graced us, once a week, with a visit. He was a front door visitor, and always had a good story to tell. For a few hours he relieved his pain, and delighted us.

Mama said when they were children he complained because they had soup every night for dinner, but he ate it anyway. In that one line statement lies his character. It was heart wrenching to see Aunt Mary's struggle, he had to do much he might have thought was women's work, but he did it anyway – with love. He deserves my best salute.

Uncle Mike's wife, Aunt Mary with Mama

3
EATING

They always had wine with their meals. In the summer, they would have chickory greens, ham or sausage with boiled eggs.

They would boil two dozen eggs. "Every now and then I would sneak into the kitchen and get one egg and bury the shell under the house. They called me the red cat."

Mama, the red cat!

Sometimes they had lonza and salami with some kind of lettuce.

For dinner, they would have some kind of soup. Chicken soup, soup made with fresh tomatoes, sometimes made with homemade noodles were a staple. Another time it would be made with noodles and English peas. Sometimes it would be made with butter beans and short cut noodles. It could be rice, with bread and some wine. No matter what, it was soup. Mike would always say he was tired of soup, but she remembered that he would eat two or three bowls full.

Their winter meals were warm, with meals like stewed chicken with Irish potatoes or stewed rabbit with potatoes and beans. They ate a lot of polenta with some kind of sauce cooked with chicken, rabbit or pigeon. On Fridays (no meat days) they would have polenta with onion. Grandma would brown the onion in a little oil, season with salt, pepper and rosemary. When this was spread over the polenta she would sprinkle parmesan cheese on top. "We had our fill. We thank God for food. It was plentiful."

After their meals Edith would ask, "What do you want to do?" It was their choice to wash dishes, dry dishes or sweep the floor.

Grandma made tomato paste. The tomatoes had to be ripe. "If a tomato was bad but one bite was good, it went into the pot." They saved all the scraps. The tomatoes were cooked for a long time, then run through a strainer. The skin and seeds were put with the other scraps for feeding the animals. Grandma put salt in the paste to preserve it. Then she put the sauce out in the sun for it to thicken. She canned all the vegetables. They would eat on them until the next crop came around.

At least once a month, they made homemade bread. Grandma would set the yeast before they went to bed. About two or three o'clock in the morning, she would get the girls up to help her. She mixed the dough, then the girls kneaded it. She broke off a piece of the dough and handed it to each child. They kneaded the dough until it was smooth. Then Grandma worked it all together and covered the dough. They would go back to bed. When they got up in the morning, they worked the dough again and made 21 or 22 large loaves of bread at a time.

Grandpa would start a fire in the brick oven he had built outdoors. If he was working in the field, Grandma would start the fire. She would move the fire from one side to the other side always checking for the same light color all over the bricks to know the oven was ready for the bread that was rising during this time. When the oven was ready Grandma would pull out all the coals and ashes with a big wet mop, clean the bottom of the oven. The mop was made just for the oven.

"They had something like a shovel but it was flat, about 10 inches wide and 15 inches long." It was just right for the bread pan. Sometimes Grandma would have a big pan with chicken and potatoes. You could smell the bread and chicken a mile from the house. "It would take about one hour for it to cook or better.

"After the bread was out of the oven, we would put the peanuts in. Ever so often, we would stir them so they would not get burned. It did not take them too long to roast. We all loved peanuts. In 1931, Lizzie made peanut brittle with raw peanuts. They sure were good. I don't know how she made that peanut brittle. She also baked cakes and candies."

Mama said they had a wood burning stove and she didn't know how Lizzie knew when the oven was ready for her to bake a cake.

When Lizzie cooked inside, nobody was allowed

in the kitchen except Edith, the watchdog. They were afraid the children would shake the floor and the cake would not rise. Mama said they could smell the cake or peanuts cooking, but if they tried to peep, Edith would slam the door on them.

She said, "Poor Lizzie."

**One of our family's picnic gatherings at Friars Point.
Mama is on the right.**

IN MEMORY OF
FRANK ANTICI

1911 – 1986

Not too long after Uncle Frank got back to the Land of the Free, after having served four years in the European Theater on the front lines, primarily in Germany, he built a new, bigger, better grocery store appropriately named Frank's Grocery. It almost encompassed the entire corner of Sixth Street and Bolivar. To the right of the store and next to the exterior stairs that led you to the living quarters grew a tree, almost into the street. In the front he had poured concrete four feet tall with steps you had to climb to get into the store. Most of his patrons would be walk-ins which was good since there was little area to park because he had built the store so big. To your right, when the door opened, manually, was Aunt Lucy's station. She was the checker, and made sure there were plenty of nickel and penny candies in great big jars on the counter. Knowing her was better than knowing Santa Claus. Using a dust rag, she wiped off every can you bought. She felt better knowing she had done her part, and you felt better knowing you had a well-dusted can. Kotex were wrapped in saved newspaper and taped. Top secret.

In the back, Uncle Frank manned the meat counter. A pound of ground beef was placed on a scale with a window on your side of the counter showing exactly how much he was weighing. He'd place the meat on waxed paper and wrap it in hardy white paper that was good for drawing on after you wiped it off a little. His homemade Italian sausage, with or without fennel, was the best – ever. At the end of the meat counter was a barrel of olives in brine with orange rind and garlic added for seasoning. Uncle Frank scooped with a net what you thought you might want, selling you direct from the barrel.

The 10 acre parking lot the local grocery store chain put in to prove their point about being big, is big. The building is even bigger. Produce department – amazing. Meat counter so big it is wrapped around both corners of the back of the store. So many interesting, delicious looking desserts you can hardly make a decision. Plus, they have speed checking out stations.

There was a day when the pendulum that is time swayed gently between simplicity and folly. In perfect harmony.

Uncle Frank during World War II, location not known. He fought on the front lines in Germany.

4

CURING

In the fall and winter, they killed hogs and a calf. Grandpa would preserve all of the meats. They cured ham, Italian sausage, salami, bacon, lonza, hoghead cheese, pickled pig feet and pickled skin.

Everything was cured with lots of salt. When the first salt would melt, Grandpa would add more salt, and finally when the salt quit melting he knew the meat was cured.

In the meat room, Grandpa put three or four big screws, with a ring on them, in the ceiling and put a wire in the ring. At the end of the wire he tied a pole the size of a hoe handle to hang the sausage and salami. There were eight or ten lengths in each strip. A fireplace in the room was kept on real low so all the grease would drain from the meats. The pole was about six feet from

46

the floor and halfway across the room. Mama said it was pretty to see those sausages hanging. The ham and bacon were on a leaning board so they could drain also. The meat was ready for eating when it quit draining.

Next she talks about hog-killing day. "There was a lot of work involved. Some of the neighbors would come and help Papa and Frank with the killing." Grandpa would return the favor when the neighbors killed their hogs. While they were working with the hogs, Grandma would be cooking a meal for all.

Hog Killing Day

First, they would lay the hog on one side in a trough. Three or four men would hold the hog while one man stabbed it in the neck. Grandma would be ready with a big pan to collect the blood when the knife was pulled out. She would sift the blood, and with her hands, work with it, adding salt, pepper, raisins and orange peeling. In no time it would gel. She would then cut slices one-half-inch thick and fry it. "We all ate it. We survived."

They didn't throw anything away except the hair and the eyes. The hooves, tongue and ears were kept. "All the children would run out in the front of the house and peep so we could watch them kill the hogs. When the hog squealed we would cover our ears and run in the house." The men would carry the hog into the building. They would tie a rope on each back leg and pull the pig up about a foot from the ground.

As soon as the pig was dead, they poured boiling water over it. With a razor sharp knife, four or five men would shave the pig. Then, starting at the throat they cut the pig open, taking out all the insides. They cut down the spine. The two halves would drain while they ate their meal.

Taking one half at a time, they cut out the ham first, the part for the lonza and then the bacon part. The rest of the meat was for sausage and salami. The small intestines were cleaned by turning them wrong side out and scrapping them with a knife. They were soaked in salty water and kept in water until the sausage and salami were made.

The big guts were used for the lonza. They would cut them open. The men would roll the meat for the lonza with the solid meat and the soft lean meat with a little fat in each piece. They rolled it tight and wrapped the big gut around it. The lonza would be 12-inches long, six- or eight-inches round, with a heavy twine wrapped around it. The twine was pulled tight, circling the lonza every two inches and then going from one end to the other about four times. It would look like a net. They fixed a loop on one end to hang the lonza.

When the girls got older, they would help make the sausage. "Frank would handle the casing. If we went too fast, he would tell us to go slower. Air between the meat would cause it to spoil. If the casing was packed too tight the guts would pop."

"We had meat until the next hog killing day came around."

Grandma made soap with the fat from the hog meat. She would add some lye, cook until thick, then cut into two-inch squares. Mama remembered that they washed their faces with the soap and also used it for shampooing their hair. It was also used to wash clothes.

IN MEMORY OF AUNT EDITH ANTICI SPAGGIARI

1913 – 1983

They were the backbone of fun. At the family gathering on July 4th, always held in Friars Point, two of my aunts would lead us in playing Cranes and Crows. Whether they invented the game or borrowed it from somebody else, we played, never knowing which way to run because they wore those two words out, stretching them to confuse us. It didn't end there. We played Pop the Whip, baseball, ate home-churned ice cream. We watched from the cool of the screened porch, the men playing bocce ball, swinging and laughing. And, coming from this group of seasoned cooks, we ate some mighty fine food. Aunt Edith led the show. I can still see those hands mixing a salad, sampling, adding a little more seasoning, sampling, until it was just right.

Like all good cooks, she had a hard time telling you exactly what she did to make something so good, but I wrestled out of her the following dish I call "Aunt Edith's Roast."

Aunt Edith's Roast

Beef chuck pot roast
garlic cloves
large can tomatoes
celery
parsley
salt and pepper
onion

Brown roast, add rest of ingredients, lower heat to 200 degrees and cook until done, when the meat can be cut with a fork. Roast at a temperature of 350 degrees.

Serve this over rice or noodles, with homemade bread, and a salad, and you'll have folks standing up and walking around their chairs, twice. That's a big thank you.

Fun-loving Eddie, Aunt Edith's only child and the eldest Antici grandchild – killed in a car accident March 1984, less than a year after her death.

5

PLAYING

They always managed to find something to play with. They would search for a toad frog, get a little twig, tap the frog on the back to make it hop and pretend it was a car. Grandma did not want them to kill toad frogs. She said they ate insects, and she wanted the children to put them in the garden.

Sometimes the family visited friends and relatives in Shelby and Jonestown, small communities nearby. "It seems like Papa was always driving fast. The top of the car was made of hard cloth. The back part would come loose from the car and stand straight out. One time Uncle Nick said, 'I am surprised you didn't lose some of your children.' We were eight in the back. Four or five sat on the seat, the other three sat on a box facing the back seat. Papa, Mama and Tony rode in front." Can you imagine eight sets of feet stepping on somebody else's feet and all the fussing that went on?

We were always together, these wonderful cousins of mine. I am second from the right.

She said of her sisters and brothers, "We had our ups and downs. Sometimes we would fight. Mama would always make us shake hands and make up or apologize." She also said if they did something Grandpa did not approve of he would tell them to go to bed without supper, but he never did that.

Over the years, Grandpa bought several cars, his first was an Ovalen purchased in 1919. Then he bought a Buick in 1923 and at least two T model Fords. One of the Fords, a brand new Turan, was purchased in

1927 for $450.00. In 1933 he bought a Nash, the last car they owned.

When Grandpa discarded one of the tires from his car the children would have some fun. "One of us would get in the tire, with our head and feet almost meeting. We would hold tight to the inside of the rim. Our brother or sister would roll the tire. It was fun until someone would roll the tire over water, or into the ditch. We took turns rolling." Whoever rolled Mama in the tire into a ditch would get the same treatment when she was the one pushing the tire.

"If Papa left an empty barrel outside, someone would get inside the barrel and we would roll them. That was not fun. The bumps and the noise were too much for them."

They played "jacks" with five little rocks and one peach bone for the ball. They always knew how to have fun. Mama recalled that they never got any toys for Christmas. They had to make up their games. They used corn cobs to make dolls. Nails were used for the eyes, nose and mouth. A piece of rag was used to wrap the cob. "That was our baby." They could not use a good rag because Grandma needed them to patch their clothes.

"We made a lot of mud pies. Didn't get dirty so Mama would not know we played with the mud."

When school was out for the summer and all the chores were finished, the children would run outside and play bare footed. Grandma and Grandpa would get chairs and sit with them in the yard. They would get some old rags and some twigs and set them on fire to keep the mosquitoes away. They would say their night prayers and run through the smoke from the fire.

When they went to bed they smelled like smoke. "Before we got into bed, Mama would tell us to brush off our feet. Well, we had to brush them with our hands. Then we would rub our hands together to shake the dust off."

Sometimes, after they ate dinner, cleaned the kitchen and finished their homework, the boys would wrestle. Grandma would laugh if Uncle Frank beat Grandpa. When the game was over, they prayed the rosary and litany and went to bed.

Grandpa taught Grandma an Italian card game called briscola. She beat him every time. She beat us all. In our version of the game the ace counts 11 points, the three counts 10 points, king is four points, queen is three points and jack is two points. They had all kinds of signals, winking one eye, pulling the ear, elbow on the table, all signals about something. Grandma's partner knew what she had and how to play. If anybody played with Grandma one on one, she would clobber you every time.

"When Papa got ready to go to town, Edith, Lena and I would run behind the brick oven and wait for him to drive by. We would run behind the car and grab the bumper. Lena would fall first. I would let go next. One time Edith went almost a block. Papa was going so fast she could not let her hands go. We would always come up with dust all over us and skinned knees."

Mama said that, when Grandpa drove, he never kept his hands in one place. His hands were always moving on the steering wheel. She explained what happened one Sunday to Edith. A lot of young boys came to their house on Sundays, and on this particular Sunday, a young man came to the house driving a T model Ford. A key wasn't needed to start the car. Mama wrote, "We drove out of the yard to the road. Edith was trying to drive like Papa, moving the wheel all the time. We were going from one side of the road to the other side. I don't know how we turned around, but Edith was driving so crazily, I jumped out right on top of a cotton stalk. Lena jumped out of the other side. It was years later before Edith drove Papa's T Model Ford."

Mama was in her late 20s the first time she heard a harmonica. Up to that time, the only music she had ever heard was Grandma singing "Ave Maria."

"We were happy, healthy and had plenty of food and lots of work. That was life."

In 1928 or 1929, Grandpa rented 40 acres of land way back in the woods. They called it "the lost 40." The men would go out there with the mules and a wagon to plow the field. When it was chopping time, Lizzie, Frank, Edith, Lena and Mama would go out to the field. Uncle Frank drove the T model Ford.

"He would always pull some kind of trick on us. We would be talking and laughing and all of a sudden he would put the brake on. We would shout, 'What happened, Frank?' He would say, 'Didn't you see that train? It crossed right in front of the car.' The only road to 'the lost 40' was a plain, narrow dirt country road. In the woods, they would holler and hear an echo. "It sure was hot. We did not feel any wind back in the woods. Sometimes we would stop to pick up some persimmons. They had to be real ripe. If not ripe, your mouth would pucker."

"When Frank said let's go, you better be ready. One time Edith wanted to pick up some more persimmons. Frank took off. Every time Edith got close to the car, Frank would take off again. He made her run a while. Next time when he said ready, we were all in the car."

They only worked 'the lost 40' for one year. It was just too much trouble.

IN MEMORY OF AUNT ANGIE ANTICI MORRIS

1918 – 1968

Louisiana's bald cypress have been wetting their feet in Missis-sippi for years, and in particular, in the Delta, and more impor-tantly, in Moon Lake, located in the northern part of the county. A 20 minute drive from Clarksdale, and closer still to my aunt's home in Friars Point. Moon Lake, all three square miles of it, holds the hope for a good day of fishing.

Aunt Angie and Aunt Edith set out one summer day along with their husbands to fish, probably for brim, using crickets as bait. They would enter the lake from the community ramp at Paradise Point in their grey looking jon boats, with trolling motors, since they weren't in a hurry. The men would go in first and the women would follow. Aunt Edith would have on a pair of Uncle Ed's cast off baggy pants, rolled up at the ankles. Her shirt would be long sleeved and the collar would be stand-ing up, protecting her neck from the sun's rays. Her well- oiled face would be sheltered by a straw hat, the kind you wear in the fields. Aunt Angie, the elegant lady in the family, sitting on the other end of the two seated boat, would be wearing below the knee cut-offs, nice looking, a white fitted blouse, sleeveless, with a possible ruffle over the shoulders. She might be wearing a visor and her shoes would be nice, compared to Aunt Edith's worn out discards. The women, fishing separate from the men, would probably be fishing in the shadows of those 50 feet tall bald cypress trees and among the knees that were protruding above the surface of the water.

The story is always varied in its telling, but it stands that this is what happened – the boat turned over. My aunts, non-swimmers, were shocked to find themselves standing in waist high water. A Power greater than I had at some point in time placed a sand bar in that very place, sparing the lives of Angie Morris and Edith Spaggiari. Recognizing their good fortune, my aunts righted the boat and began retrieving all they had lost when they heard the soft purring of a motor, the men were returning. Fearful for Uncle Tony who had suffered from angina attacks recently, Aunt Angie suggested they stand alongside the boat and hope the men wouldn't notice. When the men got close and asked if they were doing any good, the women were able to say they weren't, and they decided to call it a day. The men left, the women climbed into the boat, and it was only after they had stepped safely on shore were they able to tell the men – about the "bathing." A renewal of sorts.

Some things don't change much with time. Bald cypress trees continue to thrive in the wet of Moon Lake. On occasion you might see an eagle's nest, arm span wide, in the uppermost branches of the tree, way high in the sky. You would still slip into the lake using the community ramp and discover some lovely homes sprinkled around the edges, and you'd probably be cat fishing.

6

BATHING

"Mama made sure we all washed ourselves every night, face, arms and legs. During chopping and picking season we would be in the field late. On Saturday we took our baths. As always, we had to heat the water. In the summer, we would take our baths in the barn. One tub was for bathing, and the second tub was for rinsing ourselves. After four or five of us took our baths, we would empty the first tub and put fresh water in it. The next ones took their baths in the first rinse water and rinsed in the fresh water. We had about two or three homemade towels for all of us. The last person would put their clothes on over their damp or wet bodies." The towels would be soaked.

"In the wintertime we took our baths in the kitchen. We did not bathe every day. So much work was involved."

"Papa built a pit with bricks about 10 or 15 inches from the ground. He put four iron bars across for the big black pot to rest on. We would heat the water to wash the clothes. After we washed the white clothes, we would boil them in the pot with lye so the clothes would be pretty and white. We had a long pole to stir the clothes. After 15 or 20 minutes, we took them out, put them on a bench to drain, then washed them on a rub board and rinsed them. Before we boiled them, we had the rinse water with bluing in it ready for the last rinse. Papa bought the bluing in sticks about the size of chalk. We broke them in half, too much would make the clothes blue. One stick lasted a long time."

Sweaty clothes would soak while they ate. "After supper, Lizzie and Edith would wash the clothes while Lena, Angie and I did the dishes and cleaned the floor. We never threw the dirty dishwater away. The scraps and the dishwater would go in the hogs' trough. We never threw anything away. With the bath water we watered the garden or flowers."

"When Lizzie and Edith were through washing the clothes we would hang them out after dark. They were out all night. Sunday before lunch we would take them in."

"After Lizzie and Edith got married, Lena and I took over the washing. That was every Saturday night during the summer time. We also washed clothes during the week. Our brothers would keep our boy friends company until we finished the washings on Saturday nights.

IN MEMORY OF
THERESA ANTICI MARINELLI
1920 – 2008

The last time I saw Aunt Theresa, she was in so much pain, having broken her hip in the slightest of falls. Surgery, complications, endless pain, a hopeless situation. It would take her away from us. We would no longer hear the laughter.

Living brings problems, and she had her share, yet, she chose to make the journey with the lilt of a chuckle. An "all is well" chorus. She laughed standing up and sitting down. When visiting her, you felt refreshed. I compare the feeling to reading a book with a good ending, or seeing a movie that ends right.

Without a formal rehearsal, she had learned to live life well, to live it to the full. The doctoring, the examples, she had observed growing up, led her to know that the prize is in the race, she chose to run it – laughing.

7

DOCTORING

The first time Mama saw a doctor was when she was seven years old. When the family moved to the Sommers place, they were close to the town of Clarksdale. A Doctor Phillip was summoned to the house because Aunt Theresa had pneumonia. Mama said he was a real good person. He gave Grandma a gold cross that she gave to Mama some time in the late fifties. Mama wore that plain gold cross a lot. Under her holographic Will, Mama gave the cross to Mary Ann as a gift but we could not find it. What a loss.

Dr. Phillip must have been kind to all of them. Mama said they were always glad to see him. He was special to them. I have tried to learn his whole name and where he served in the area but have had no luck.

For the most part Grandma and Grandpa took care of the children's problems. For winter coughs, Grandpa heated wine and added a lot of black pepper to it. The children drank it hot and hiccupped for what seemed like ten minutes. Then, he sent them straight to bed. They would get so hot it didn't seem like wintertime, but "It would break that cough."

For a bad cold, Grandma boiled hog hoof and made a tea with it for the children to drink. First, she scraped the hoof real well, left it in water overnight and then, washed it several times. Once dried it was ready for "bad-cold" tea. Grandma also put Vicks vapor rub on their chests and covered them with a heavy flannel blanket. At night, the Vicks was soothing, and the children were warmed by the tea and blanket. In the daytime they kept their clothes up to the neck so they wouldn't get cold. Two generations later, Vicks is still used at our house for winter colds.

For a sore back or a bad sprain, Grandma made a paste from sulphur, smoothed it onto a thick cloth and wrapped up the sore spot. Everything Grandpa and Grandma did worked. When the children had a bad cut, Grandma washed the wound with kerosene to stop the bleeding. She put a clean cloth over the cut to keep dirt out. If the cut was deep, she washed it with kerosene, and then, put sugar on it to stop the bleeding. The next day she washed with kerosene again to keep infection out. "It worked every time."

The children had all common diseases such as measles, chicken pox, roseola and mumps. Some had pneumonia. Uncle Mike had diphtheria. He was quarantined in Grandma's room. Mama remembered that they could not go into the room, and that Grandma kept his plate and silverware separate from the rest of the family. Apparently, Grandma didn't have a cure for him because she said the doctor took care of him.

One day Grandma was bitten by a black widow spider when she was using the toilet. Grandpa went for the doctor because her side was getting numb. Thank God, with the doctor and medicine, she recovered. "We all had to pitch in and help – add a little more to our daily jobs."

IN MEMORY OF
TONY ANTICI

1924 – 1990

A picture of Uncle Tony hung in the house on Iowa, in a prominent place, a picture of the son who had graduated from eighth grade. He was dressed in a white suit, holding a diploma in his hands, and smiling. He was their youngest child and he had accomplished what none of the eight before him had done. He had completed all that had been offered to him.

For his parents, illiterates, foreigners to the land in which he was born, it was an accomplishment indeed. He didn't let them down.

When he was 20, still living with his parents, his oldest sister died. There were two children left without parents. One would come to live with him and his parents. When he proposed to my aunt, he told her he had a son. They would raise him in their home which grew with five more children, all boys.

He would be a farmer, a fine farmer, a church leader, a respected man. He did not disappoint. He had been schooled well.

69

Uncle Tony's 8th Grade Graduation

8

SCHOOLING

There was a big hailstorm in the spring of 1919 when Mama was only five years old. Her memory is very clear about that event. The three older children were at school, and those at home were hiding behind a door in the bedroom. Mama was holding Angie, who at that time, was around six months old. They were all afraid of the storm. A strong wind blew out the glass from the only window on the side of the house where the storm was coming from. Grandma's cutting board was used to cover the window preventing rain and hail from coming into the house. Grandpa had to brace himself between the two iron beds to keep the board on the window. After the storm died down, Grandpa got the mule and wagon and rushed to the school to get the older children. Mama was too young to attend school in 1919.

Grandma had a lot of cleaning to do and the three young children, Mama being one of them, walked out on the porch to see the hail. It was four or five inches deep, but on the side, where the wind was so strong, it was seven inches deep. In all of my years I have never seen hail stacked like what she described. That was one powerful storm.

I have read the journal numerous times, and I am always amazed by Mama's exactness in describing things. A child of five years saw hail stacked seven inches deep. I believe it was her "eye" for detail that enabled her years later to be the marvelous seamstress she became.

The children loved the hail. It was like candy to them. They had never seen ice like that.

In the fall of 1923, the family moved to a large house close to a school. John Sommers, Sr. owned the building and operated his farm from there. He allowed them to use one big room for the school. All grades were in that one room with the younger children sitting in front and the older children sitting in the back. "We did not have kindergarten, school began with first grade. Each grade was separate. This is the first school I remember."

She must mean that this was the first school she attended. She was nine years old.

In the fall, when school started, the children went only in the morning. After lunch they picked cotton. Toward the end of October, they started going to school all day. In the spring, they went for half a day because they had to chop cotton. School sessions were short because the children had to help make a living for the family. She said, "I liked arithmetic. I liked to work with numbers."

At school they learned how to play baseball, but she didn't remember what kind of bat or ball they had. She said, "It was fun." Sometimes they played "Pop the Whip." "The last one would roll in the field." Mama said the school was an abandoned house at the end of the field Grandpa was working on.

This must have been a different school from the one on the Sommers Place.

During those years of Mama's young schooling, children of Italian immigrants went to a school for them only. If it seems insulting, it was not. Those children could not have fit into a regular public school. All their garments were homemade. They did not have enough shoes for all the children. And while they were not dirty, they did not look like city children.

Mama mentioned only once in the journal that there was some discrimination against the Italian people.

"Later years, we had a little mixture, but we never had black children. There were quite a few black families out on the farm. They were working for the man who owned the land as day labors."

Once a month, a nurse from the Health Clinic would come to the school. Mama was in her early teens before the nurse told the students they needed to brush their teeth. Then, she gave all of them a tooth brush and baking soda to use to brush their teeth.

The nurse said Mama's tonsils were bad. In the winter of 1923, Mama, Frank and John Sabbatini had their tonsils removed. Mama said she put up a big fight. "Papa had to help the doctor and nurse hold me down. I don't know how many days we stayed in the hospital."

The health nurse visited Mama in the hospital and asked her if she could get her anything. The first thing Mama saw were red beads the nurse was wearing, and she told her she wanted beads like hers. The nurse took her necklace off and gave it to Mama. They were a long string of faceted red plastic beads, and Mama loved them and took care of them.

The three children recovered from the tonsillectomies. "We had to stay home one week. Then we went back to school. We loved going to school. Mrs. Wood was our teacher. She was old. The second year Mrs. Wood's daughter, Mrs. McKenny, started teaching us. She was a pretty lady."

In 1928, a new schoolhouse was built. "There were no windows on the west side, that was for the blackboard. There were windows on the east side, that's where the desks were, a front door and a back door. We had a wood burning heater at one end of the building. The school was about one mile from our house." Italians couldn't go to public school. County schools ended in eighth grade. Years later, they could go to city school and graduate from twelfth grade.

"In the wintertime, we wore a knit cap on our heads. We had no over shoes, no gloves, no raincoat. One morning Edith's hair was sticking up. She wet her hair and put on her cap. When we got to school, the hair that was out of her cap had ice on it. We walked facing the north wind, and sometimes, it was so cold our faces would be red and our hands and feet would be stiff."

"When it was raining, we would run home. Mama (Grandma) would be at the back door waiting for us with tears in her eyes. We got caught in the rain quite a few times." Mama said she didn't know where Grandpa and the car were. Wherever he was, he was probably driving fast.

Mama recalled a storm that happened during school. "Our teacher, Mrs. Williams, made everybody get away from the windows, into the middle of the building. She told us to be calm, and if it got bad, we would run out and jump in the ditch."

A teacher from Friars Point, around 30 miles north of Clarksdale, had to jump that very ditch to get to the school building.

"In 1929, our baseball team played Herrin High team. Our team was Bramlett High. Our boys won the game." That was the first time she saw my daddy – at the ball game. She said he was skinny with big ears.

IN MEMORY OF
ENRICA (RITA) ANTICI FURINI,
MY MOTHER
1914 – 2002

I am sitting on my mother's lap, too small to sit on the chair alone. The teacher takes my hand and places it on the wheel that will make the needle go into the fabric, creating the first seam. We are making a child's apron with a pocket, small, for my little hand. She tells me that we will embroider butterflies and flowers on the finished apron, in cross stitch, of course, simple stitches I can do. As we begin sewing, I can feel the rhythm, sitting on her lap, as she motors the foot pedal. Up and down, up and down. It's a good feeling. I am hooked on sewing.

Beginning when we were very small, Mama made all of our clothes, pedaling away on her Singer sewing machine. She purchased paisley printed flour sacks from Delta Wholesale Hardware Store on Sunflower, near the railroad tracks. She made her own patterns, altering as needed for each of us. We had new outfits for every occasion. Little girls had handmade aprons. Real dolls had doll clothes. When Mildred got married, her husband upgraded my mother's machine to an electric, and she whizzed along, refining her talent, using better materials.

My mother, Rita, became a sought after seamstress. She worked until she was in her late 70s, and then continued altering for friends even after she had retired. The talents she had learned as a young lady became survival for her and for us. They multiplied and became her livelihood. More than anything else, she taught us by her example to be grateful for the gifts God places in our lives, to use them, to share them, to pass them on.

9

CLOTHING AND SEWING

"We never did go up town to shop for clothes or shoes until we were in our mid teens. Papa would buy three or four pairs of shoes. He would give each of us a pair of shoes. If they fit, fine. If they did not fit, it was still fine. We had to wear them." Their shoes were always high tops with seven or eight eyes.

Mama also remembered that they at one time had one pair of high top dress shoes with five buttons on the side. "One Sunday I'd wear the shoes, the next Sunday Lena would wear them. Let me tell you, they were not my size. They hurt my feet."

Grandma made their dresses, also their slips and bloomers. When the girls reached puberty, she made their bras. The bras were a flat piece of cloth with a strap and one snap.

When they did go into town, there were only two dry good stores, and a grocery store sat between them. Mrs. Rose Kantor and Mrs. Fannie Levine operated the dry good stores. Pete Bolgeo had the grocery store and he got all the business until Joe Noe, Sr. opened a grocery store and service station on the corner of Fourth Street and Sunflower. He sold gas for 15 cents a gallon.

There was only one bridge crossing the Sunflower River to get to town. That bridge, the Fourth Street Bridge, (now called Martin Luther King, Jr. Bridge) was built down in the bank of the river. "We had to go down the bridge and up on the other side. I was always afraid when we were crossing the bridge. We had to stop on the other end. The car would roll back down the bridge. It took good brakes to keep the car from rolling back."

In the late 20s, the Second Street Bridge was built and in the 40s or 50s, the First Street Bridge was built. Those two bridges were even with the street. They tore down the Fourth Street Bridge and built it up to what it is today. Mama also said they redid the Second Street Bridge to include a place for people to walk across.

They had no house shoes, house slippers, house coat or robe. There were no rugs on the floors of their house. In the wintertime, when it was real cold, they sat close together around the fireplace. At bedtime they took off their shoes and stockings and left them close to the fire. They would run into their room, put on their homemade gowns and jump into beds which had already been heated with a warmer. For a while the beds would be warm and cozy, but when the temperatures dropped close to zero, it would be cold in the house and the beds would cool down.

In the morning the bedroom would be so cold, they would jump into their clothes as fast as they could and then rush to the main room where the fireplace was roaring to put on their stockings and shoes. They had to put on coats and caps to go to the outhouse. Shaking all the way, they then had to wash their face and hands on the back porch before gathering again around the fireplace.

When the children were young, Grandma combed their hair straight back and tied it in the back. Grandma wore her hair that way except she twisted it around into a bun at the nape of her neck. We called it a choo-choo.

As the children got older, she cut their hair so they could comb it themselves. She would tell them to pick up the hair off the floor or a toad frog would make his nest in it and they would get a headache. That was a good way to make them clean up. They must have believed her. "Everything they did worked so why take a chance with the hair. We would later burn the hair in the pit.

"When we got to a certain age, Mama would make us start working on our trousseau. Papa would buy a big roll of material to make bed sheets. We would have to measure it, make sure it would be 108 inches long. We would pull one thread across the 80 inches wide and cut where we pulled the thread. We sewed a three-inch hem at the top and a one and one/half-inch hem at the bottom."

"Lena and I would work together. We cut four top sheets first, then four bottom sheets. Pull the thread across before we cut each sheet. The bottom sheet was shorter than the top. We had to make sure there was enough material to tuck under the mattress all around. We would center the top sheet, pick the design we wanted, fix the pattern right over the sheet so many inches from the hem. Make sure the center on the sheet and pattern match. Put cloth over the pattern with a hot iron, then stamp design on the sheets and pillow cases. The pillow cases we made were six or eight inches longer than the ones we use today, and not as wide. When we finished the embroidery, we crocheted the lace on the end of the hem. Sometimes the lace was two or three inches deep – so pretty. That is why we started early."

They made everything for their trousseau, which included two dresses, their sleeping gowns, slips and underwear. Mama said, "You name it, we cut and sewed it." It would take over a year, maybe two, to complete all they made. They made all the towels and crocheted lace one-inch deep on the face towels. They embroidered designs, mostly flowers, in the corner of the towels and on the edges of the pillow cases.

They had some extra material and decided to make napkins. Mama embroidered an "N" for napkin on hers. She said later, "I still have my napkins with "N" embroidering."

None of the girls used lipstick, rouge or powder. As they grew older, they learned a lot of things to help take care of their health and their looks. Lizzie parted her hair in three parts. The top part was pulled back.

The side would be pushed forward like muffs over her ears. She bought hairpins for her sisters. "Lizzie bought tweezers to pluck her eyebrows. She also used some kind of liquid to clean her face." They all had pencil thin eyebrows so they must have followed her in everything.

Back then signs on the highway must have been made of some kind of material and stamped with logos. A Mrs. Spaggiari gave Grandma a lot of strips of this cloth. There was paint and writing on the material so they bleached it. They soaked the material in water with some ashes over night. The next day, they washed it again, rubbed it on the rub board and hung the strips on the clothes line. As soon as they were dry they would dip them in water and hang them back on the line. She said they did this five or six times a day until the strips were bleached white. It took about four weeks to complete the bleaching process. Then they put them in hot water with lye, boiled them a while and rinsed the material in bluing water with the result being very white pieces of material.

Mama devotes pages to sewing. She cut out long strips for curtains and then cut smaller strips for ruffles. She also made a valance with ruffles. She dyed the ruffle for the boys room a blue color. In the girls room the ruffle was pink, the next room was yellow and Grandma and Grandpa's room had a green ruffle. They had a pedal sewing machine and of course it had no tool for making ruffles. Mama had to work slowly ruffling the material as she went along. She said it was hard work and took a lot of patience. "It took me a few days to finish them," she said.

The finished curtains had to be starched and ironed before they could be hung in the various rooms. Everybody was pleased with them. Mama was 17 at the time.

Surely the curtains were made for their new home, the White House, and that is why she remembered every detail. I don't know what she used for coloring the material – I do know that they dyed eggs with natural things.

Mama wrote that when she sewed, "There is no telling how many miles I pedaled a day using both feet on the pedal to have better control of the machine."

Mama made BVD's for the men. "I had no pattern. I looked at and measured some Mama and Lizzie had made. They were one piece with an opening in the back. The flap was secured by a button to keep it closed. The front buttoned from the neck to the crotch. There were seven or eight buttons in front, and we sewed all the button holes by hand." She said the legs were four or five inches long.

When she was 20, she began to cut and sew shirts for the family to wear in the field. Again, she had no pattern. She looked at the men's shirts and cut out the material. What she particularly remembered were all the button holes that were sewn by hand.

IN MEMORY OF AUNT LIZZIE ANTICI BARBIERI

1910 – 1944

If the end times had happened that night, my sisters and I would have been some of the first to be snatched up, lying out in the front yard looking skyward for constellations. We were in search of the Bear, the Lion, the Hunter. What we saw were shooting stars making a once in a lifetime showing, just for us. We were frightened. With all the talk about living a good life, always being ready, there we were, caught in the middle of the beginning of the end. It was spectacular, beyond belief. I have never forgotten the excitement.

Some serious things happened to our family in the 40s, two tragedies. Uncle Joe Barbieri died on Christmas day, 1942, from cancer, and his wife, my Aunt Lizzie, died in November, 1944, from cancer as well. They had two small children; the family would circle around them trying to close the gap.

I was too young to remember my aunt, and yet, I remember where she lived. I know that it was a white apartment on top of a garage. It was in an alley.

85

In like manner, I can remember that we lived on Jefferson the night of the extravaganza, but not the year, or season. I see no harm in thinking that maybe, just maybe, the stars were proclaiming two new arrivals, two young souls entering the pearly gates.

**Aunt Lizzie with her children,
Mary Ann and Louis**

10

THE WHITE HOUSE

In 1928, Grandpa bought 80 acres of land west of Clarksdale and had a big house built on the land. In 1930, when Mama was 16, it was completed, and the family of eleven moved into the new house, the White House. Mama said, "It really stood out – the only white house in the country."

The house had four bedrooms, a living room, dining room and a kitchen. It also had a wine cellar for Grandpa's homemade peach wine, and they stored potatoes and other vegetables there too. It had a bath room with no fixtures so it was used for a storage room. The hall was the length of the house, separating bedrooms from the living part of the house. There was one front door and one back door and a large porch on the front with a smaller porch in the back. All around the front porch they built a wall two feet high and 10 inches wide. She recalled how nice it was to sit on that front porch. On the back porch there was one board 10 inches wide from the house to the post where a bucket of water with a dipper was placed as well as a face pan. The towel was hung from a nail on the board. "If we did some kind of work outside we better wash our hands before coming into the house."

Originally there was an old house where the new house was built. That house, the old house, was moved way back from the new house and Grandpa and Uncle Frank built a fence around it, eventually enclosing the entire area. They took the floor off two of the rooms for the mules to eat and be out of the weather. The hogs went under the house. There were three rooms left for storage. One of those rooms was used in the winter as a meat processing room. The other two rooms were used for storing hay for the mules to eat during the winter.

Since the White House was bigger there were more household chores.

When they washed, it would take three or four hours washing on a rub board. There would be five sets of sheets from five double beds and one set from a single bed, plus pillow cases. They would wash dish towels, face towels, bath towels and the clothes for 11 people. They soaked two sheets at a time and had to wring them by hand. While the sheets were drying on the lines, they washed towels and their clothes. She said that they washed outside always and it was not fun. But the hard part was to come.

"Washing was hard but ironing was worse. In the winter it was fine because the iron kept you warm. In the summer time you were very hot." They would have a fire in the fireplace with two solid irons weighing three or four pounds each in front of the fire. When one iron got cool you put it in front of the red coals and picked up the next one. They would iron all day. They starched the white shirts the men wore.

Mama said when they had to iron the curtains it would take two days. They had 13 long windows, three short windows and curtains for the front door and back door. She cut and sewed all those curtains.

They worked hard and played hard. When they were in their teens they would have a watermelon wash on Saturday nights. In June, when the harvest was plentiful, they would invite friends over to eat watermelon. At some point, one person would plant a watermelon slice on somebody's head, and then, they all would be chasing and screaming and wearing watermelon. Everybody would come to the White House. She said they all danced on the front porch.

There were dances at the Italian American Club too. It was built very near the school and about a mile from their home. It still stands today, but is in very bad shape.

One evening Frank and two of his friends were going to the club. Mama and Aunt Lena were riding with Edith and Lizzie and their boyfriends in another car. They were "the chaperones" and were really enjoying themselves. Frank was driving pretty fast, and all of a sudden he sped straight up to the car Mama was riding in. They were scared to death! Of course, he stopped – with inches to spare and laughing at their fright. When it was all over, Frank said a little toy car could fit between the cars.

Italian-American Club, shabby but still standing.

Mama called him and his buddies the Three Mus-
keteers – they were always together. Frank was only 17
and had no driver's license. In fact, none of them had
driver's licenses. "The cars back then had a brake and
a clutch. You kept your feet over both of them. When
you stropped you pressed both feet. The clutch kept
the motor running. There were no gears to shift. You
had one lever, push it down to go and pull up to stop."

You can tell in the journal how proud Mama was
of the White House. The family was living proof that
much can be attained if you try. Grandpa came to this
country in 1904 penniless. It took him two years to
pay off the debt for the boat fare. He married, lived
in shacks, but was never hungry. In the late 1920s, he
owned land, built a house, had a car, and was well on
his way to raising his nine children. They never lost
their faith, and in 1930, when they walked into their
new home, the White House, they were slap dab in the

middle of the American Dream. The nine children grew up to be good people who added to their community in many ways and who remained faithful to their religious beliefs. Grandma and Grandpa would outlive two of their nine children. Lizzie died in 1944 from cancer, and Angie died in 1968 from cancer as well.

The family lived in the White House for eight years before selling the house and the farm. The house was moved, but when Mama and I drove out to their old homestead one summer day the brick oven was still there. We walked around as she remembered where things had been. There were some rose bushes near where the house had stood, and we cut a few of the small pink roses to bring home. Mama was full of memories of days gone by.

**Mama on right with her beloved Frank and Lena
in the mid 30s.**

IN MEMORY OF
GRANDFATHER FILIPPO ANTICI

1880 – 1969

While resting in the semi-shade offered by the backyard pergola with Carolina jasmine hanging from its uppermost rafters, I see a small yellow crop dusting plane, flying low, seems like he dipped his right wing at me, a signal that the scenery is going to be changing. I knew he was up to no good when I started smelling defoliant.

This had to happen. The cotton is bursting at its seams, so lovely I can compare it to fresh fallen snow with no paw prints on it, not one. We'll need to ride the countryside and enjoy the beauty for a few days longer because the six row pickers can go through a field while you're getting a shower, catching you by surprise.

My grandfather had two mules named Fannie and Tom to pull the plow so he could plant. He had nine pickers, his children, to help with the harvesting. No matter the difference, those who work the land are subject to nature.

The hail that my mother saw stacked seven inches deep probably ruined a crop. It might have denied a child a pair of shoes.

Today, even with irrigation pumps and watering sprinklers that can cover 140 acres at a time, the blistering winds can wither young plants in a day. And, of course, there is always the problem of too much water.

We know that endings have beginnings. Sometimes it takes a season to see better times, sometimes it takes a lifetime. Grandpa, with pipe hanging out of the corner of his mouth and a thumb blackened from pushing the tobacco into the bowl, knew about endings, and he knew about beginnings, the sweet taste that accompanies endurance.

11
ENDING

Some time in the summer of 1930 a man asked Mama's parents for her hand. He wanted her for his wife. They must have said yes. She questioned why her parents had done that. He didn't ask Mama to be his girlfriend, he just gave her an engagement ring. Not only did she not love him, she thought he was too jealous. She loved to dance; he didn't want her dancing with anyone else. She enjoyed being with lots of different girls and boys; he did not.

In the spring of 1931, Mama finally broke the engagement and gave him back the ring. He begged her to keep it, but she knew if she did he would continue to tell people she was his girlfriend.

That fall she began her first year at Herrin High as an eighth grader. The same young man came to the school every day to see her on her lunch hour. She was tired of seeing him and dropped out of school just before exams. She told Grandma and Grandpa she wasn't going to school anymore. She would rather stay home and chop cotton than have to see him everyday. She was 17 years old.

Several boys asked her to go steady with them, but she didn't want to be tied down. She wanted to enjoy her young life. She remembered one man who could sing and yodel. She said you could hear him from a mile away.

"It was fun to be free and do as I pleased, but after a while I thought it was time to settle down."

Daddy, the skinny man with the big ears, began courting her. They dated for two years before getting engaged on September 22, 1935. "After I got engaged to Guaito, Papa bought my trunk. I placed my trousseau in it. I put the best set of sheets and pillow cases on top for our first night together. Mama bought me two silk gowns. I still have the worn out gown I wore on my honeymoon, from my house to his house. HaHa. We moved in with his family. I was not happy to live with his family. But that was that."

In June of 1936, they had moved out of the Furini house, with Mama pregnant with Mildred and moved into the building that at one time was Herrin High, where daddy went to school. Daddy bought a three-eyed kerosene cook stove. He bought a little oven to put over one eye to bake bread. I would love to know more about that oven.

She said that she used the kerosene cook top until 1942 when they got a gas stove. They also bought a hot water tank that she later sold to Agnes Hood when we moved to Monroe Circle.

Daddy got a job working at Liberty Cash grocery store and Mama picked and chopped cotton on her family's place.

The early part of December 1936, Mama and Daddy moved up town on Jefferson. "What a difference. Lights in every room. Toilet in the house. Running water in the house."

This was her first experience living in a town.

Grandpa Furini had given them $500, and they bought a coupe car with some of the money. With the rest they bought food.

Mama cut and sewed all the clothes for her first baby. She would drive the coupe by herself to her parents house, sew the clothes, and then, make button holes and sew little buttons on the garments at home. "I had never driven a car before then." That might explain why she said she always parked the car in the same place when she got home.

The house Mama and Daddy lived in on Jefferson is called a shot gun house in the Delta. It has two nice sized rooms, a small kitchen and a bath room. Mildred was born in that house around eight o'clock a.m. on December 31, 1936. They were still living there when Mary Ann was born on October 26, 1938.

In the spring of 1939 the family of four moved to Greenwood. They had to rush to Clarksdale for my birth in May of 1940. Raymond was born on March 8, 1943. We were both born in the old Clarksdale hospital which now is a doctor's office.

The journal doesn't say when they moved back to

Clarksdale, but it was sometime between 1940 and 1943. They moved again on Jefferson into the house of my early memories. The house was owned by Miss Agnes Hood, a wonderful older lady, who took a liking to us children and to Mama.

The last entry in Mama's journal is dated August 4, 1999.

Beginning on July 13, 1992, she had recorded 87 pages of family history beginning with her birth. She had shared with us their love and respect for each other, their hard work planting and gathering in the crops, their poor living conditions, their prayer life and their happiness.

It was the one line entry at the end that tears at our hearts because we can only imagine the pain she endured on that day.

"Guaito walked out of our lives on December 30, 1943, 12 days before our eighth wedding anniversary."

What she meant was that Daddy packed his belongings and left her and the four children that night.

A NEW BEGINNING

Do what is right and good
in the sight of the Lord.
Deuteronomy 6: 18.

Mama and the four children.
I am the blonde.

My brother Raymond.
His head was full of curls.

**Raymond, Mildred, Mary Ann and Jo Ann
in the 40s.**

12

STARTING OVER

Mama certainly had to have a lot on her mind that evening before the last day of the year, 1943. At the age of 29, she was alone with four children, the youngest only nine months old, and being born severely club footed was in need of medical attention. Her talents were simple ones. She knew how to live the life of a farmer's wife, and she knew how to sew. The rent and utilities would need to be paid and she had to provide food for us.

I am sure she cried a lot, but I never saw a tear until later years.

Enrica, Mama, had to hold on tightly to her faith and inner strength to keep us all going. Along the way she forgave, accepted the hand dealt her, circled us with love and affection and always, always was there for us through everything.

In less than a year, she would lose her oldest sister,

Lizzie, to cancer. That was a tremendous blow to all the family especially the girls who looked up to her. Mama said she "led the way for them." To her it was like losing a mother because Lizzie had in fact been mother to them all as Grandma helped make the living.

Mama was strict, but I don't say that as a three year old. I just know that from the first day I can remember she was strict. We didn't have to walk a chalk line, but if we disobeyed her, a spanking followed immediately.

And, as regular as morning and night, we prayed daily as a family, especially the rosary.

We continued living on Jefferson Street, which, even then, was not the best part of town. Blacks and whites got along fine with white folks living on one side of the street and blacks living on the other side. Mama would be friends to all.

As a small child Raymond, developed polio that affected one of his legs. Mama had to leave him in Memphis for weeks at a time while doctors tried to help him gain strength in the leg. She had to ride the bus to Memphis with him and me, also born with one foot twisted, to Campbell's Clinic for corrective shoes. I don't know how she managed, but with the help of her family, we were fed and sheltered. Mama put her talent with sewing to work and made our clothes, dressing the three girls so we looked like triplets.

In the 50s, the housing authority built apartments for the needy and Mama applied. We thought we were in high cotton when we moved into our new apartment. The two older girls got married and Mama, my brother and me lived there until our combined salaries prohibited us staying any longer.

Mama moved a few more times as her needs were reduced by my brother leaving home and also my marriage in 1964.

She remained close to her family – they were her best friends – and close to the church. I believe we went to every service offered, including confessions every Saturday afternoon.

We had no car. She had to depend on the kindness of her family to get us where we needed to go. And, we walked a lot, going to town and to visit the relatives.

Mama learned never to waist a penny. Somehow, she saved enough to travel to numerous places in the States and also abroad. She went to Italy twice, and on the second trip, had a chance to meet some of Grandpa's nieces and nephew. Fluent in Italian, she was able to visit the courthouse and gather information about Grandpa's family. She visited the graves of some relatives and was even able to go into Grandpa's home in Ostra and walk around and think about his life before he came to America.

Mama never strayed from the family, was always there when we needed her and always ready to help in any way she could. She devoted her life to God and family and never lost track of where she was headed.

Being without material possessions became second nature to her, she never splurged on anything, unless you count cigarettes, and at her death in 2002, she left us a lovely monetary gift as well as a few treasures we cherish to this day.

TREASURES

For where your treasure is,
there also will your heart be.
Matthew 6: 21.

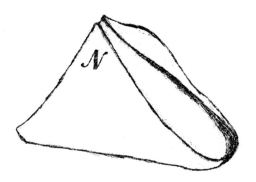

Napkin with an "N" on it.

13

THE RED BEADS

Mama wore very little makeup. Her eyebrows were pencil thin. She wore a loose powder by Coty that you can still buy, a little rouge and lipstick. I keep an open container of the powder in my clothes closet. It smells so good and reminds me of her.

As she got older, her clothes were more tailored and she liked bright colors. She said when you get older you need to do things to brighten yourself up. She enjoyed a few pieces of jewelry, wore them daily even when she retired. Among her favorites were the gold cross, some opal earrings, the diamond watch Raymond had given her years earlier, and Grandma's engagement ring worn on the middle finger of her right hand.

Taking the red beads from the necklace she had received when her tonsils were removed, we had earrings made for each of the children and grandchildren. Also, the beads from the necklace she wore on her wedding day were made into earrings for all of us. Those beads were light blue sparkling crystal.

When we were going through her things, we came upon the napkins (the ones with the "N" in the corner) and were puzzled. It was only after reading the journal that we laughed as we knew she did when she wrote it. "N" for napkin. We each have one, and I pull mine out for every gathering of family and to myself or out loud, I say, "Mama showed up." Somehow it doesn't feel quite so empty without her.

The same Mama who had so few material possessions was the same Mama who saved every note we ever sent her. She even had the spiritual bouquet I gave her when I was in elementary school. I imagine those gifts were precious because she received so few. I am so glad we all lived long enough to tell her we appreciated all she had done for us.

Mama had reminders of the week we celebrated her birthday for a whole week, every day doing something different and ending with grilled steak on the last night.

One year we took her shopping in Memphis and bought her several new outfits. That was new for her and she dearly loved it. She got a few things she would not have spent her money on.

The hand crafted rosary was such a joy to her. Mary Ann and Mildred had written on a piece of paper the names of her parents, sisters and brothers, our names and our children's names, so as she prayed she had a name to specifically pray for. And the fact that each bead was a birth gem really made it special.

But the present that meant the most to her, I think, was the huge stocking we filled for her one Christmas. It cost us an arm and a leg to fill that thing but it was worth every dollar spent. We shopped. We bought. We even got the page from the newspaper for the date she was born, and she loved it. There were games and fun things as well. And you always, as in always, gave her Chantilly dusting powder for Christmas. It was in the stocking.

When you read Mama's journal you can see over and over again how much she loved and respected her parents and siblings. Our lives were filled with love for family also. All the grandchildren loved Grandpa because he was so much fun. He taught us a lot of Italian words and insisted that we all learn to count to 10 in Italian. And he always wanted us to sample his home brewed peach wine.

Whenever you left their home he always said, "God bless you. God bless me. God bless America." He loved this country.

It was only after his death in 1969 that we had the opportunity to pay attention to Grandma and learn what a precious spirit she had. Grandma laughed so easily. On her 1942 "Alien Registration Card" her height is listed as five feet, three inches and her weight as 175 pounds. We always said she was five by five, and she was.

Neither she nor Grandpa ever became citizens of the United States because they could not read or write. Grandma could read printed Italian, but that was of no help with English. The children taught Grandpa how to write his name so he could sign checks. The problem was that he placed no significance on the order of the letters, and they finally gave up.

Grandma and Grandpa loved this country, though. One of their sons fought on the front lines in Europe during World War II and several cousins served in the military in Korea and Vietnam.

When I was first married, they lived on Sixth Street close to Uncle Frank's store. We would walk in the yard past the side of their house and peep in the kitchen window. Quite often they would be sitting on that old green divan, holding hands, watching some program on their black and white television. Grandpa really loved boxing. He would be making all the motions, really getting involved in the fight. You didn't know whether to watch the fight or watch him.

Their kitchen/den was at the back of the house so you would go in from the back door. Grandma and Grandpa continued to have a garden, and you might see a box with a string set to trap some unsuspecting bird. They knew their birds and how to clean them, and Grandma could smell up the neighborhood with her cooking.

Later, they moved from Sixth Street to their final home on Florence Avenue. Grandpa died of a heart attack in 1969, and Grandma died in 1981.

I did not know when I asked for Grandma's well-worn black leather prayer book after her death – what a treasure I held in my hands. It was only after reading the journal, that I realized it was Grandma's most personal earthly possession.

Mama gave us a lifetime of treasures. We learned to cook, to sew, embroider, crochet. We learned to pray, to be faithful, to love family. We learned that you didn't have to have material things to be content. She taught us by her example to always strive to do what is right and good.

And while this isn't important, I do love her plastic Blue Bonnet butter container. And I love the plate we ate polenta out of. I am so glad to have the embroidered pieces we made as children and the crochet doilies – she saved them all.

Over time, I have come to realize that Mama was able to endure because she had been formed so well. The family had wonderful work ethics. Work was distributed according to age and ability. They had to work the garden to be able to eat. They had to feed the animals and water the mules and make butter. They had to chop the cotton from sun up to sun down and pick the cotton, and chop wood, and harvest the corn and sugar cane. She knew from experience that if you keep doing what is right you will succeed. She lived that life until the day she died.

My grandparents gave us the gift of this country and our faith, my mother remained faithful. I applaud all of them.

Mama's words, "I have lived a good life – all because of my faith."

ATTI DI MORTE

L'anno mille novecento *diciasette*, addì *sei*, di *marzo* a ore *undici* e minuti *due*, nella Casa Comunale.
Avanti di me *Cavalier Italo Antolini, Sindaco*

Uffiziale dello Stato Civile del Comune di *Ostra* sono comparsi *Ferro Pietro*, di anni *cinquantacinque*, *contadino* domiciliato in *Ostra*, e *Sartini Vincenzo*, di anni *quarantacinque* *contadino*, domiciliato in *Ostra*, i quali mi hanno dichiarato che a ore *diciotto* e minuti *quindici* di *ieri*, nella casa posta in *contrada S. Giacomo* al numero *625.1*, è morto *Antici Antonio* di anni *sessantatre*, *contadino* residente in *Ostra* nato in *Ostra il 11-2-1854*, da *Domenico*, domiciliato in ____, e da *fu Marcellini Rosa*, domiciliata in ____, *vedovo di Pacenti Teresa*
A quest'atto sono stati presenti quali testimoni *Ventura Antonio Marino*, di anni *sessanta*, *impiegato*, e *Croci Silvio*, di anni *cinquantanove*, *impiegato*, ambi residenti in questo Comune. Letto il presente atto a tutti gl'intervenuti, *meno li sottoscrivono i testimoni sol tanto, avendo il dichiarante asserito di essere analfabeti.*
Ventura Antonio Marino
Silvio Croci
Italo Antolini Sindaco

Numero *35*

Antici Antonio
fu Domenico

**Death certificate of Antonio Antici, Grandpa's father.
Mama got this from the courthouse in Ostra.**

THE LETTER

> What I am so thankful for
>
> I thank all of you for what you did for me when I was down but not out. I thank you for your kindness and respect, but most of all your love. It was my deep love for you, that I was able to keep my spirit up, when time was hard and rough. Money was short, I could not have done it with out the help from God. The Lord gave me strenth, lift up my spirit open my mind and cleared my sight, so I could see and know what was best for all of us. I have come a long way in my old age. First I thank God for guiding me, and leading me on the right path, I am so thankful for the deep love I have for God. It was my parents who taught me this deep love for God. I hope my life was a good example for you, I love each one of you, I pray you never loose faith in God. He is the only one who can help you. I love you so much, It was you who kept me going. You stayed by my side through

Copy of portion of handwritten letter.

113

14

THE LAST LETTER

My mother wrote an undated letter to us and stored it in her bank lock box. We opened it after her death and I have copied it unaltered for your reading.

"I thank all of you for what you did for me when I was down but not out. I thank you for your kindness and respect but most of all your love. It was my deep love for you that I was able to keep my spirit up when time was hard and rough, money was short. I could not have done it without the help from God. The Lord gave me strength, lift up my spirit, open my mind and cleared my sight so I could see and know what was best for all of us. I have come a long way in my old age.

First, I thank God for guiding me and leading

me on the right path. I am so thankful for the deep love I have for God. It was my parents who taught me this deep love for God. I hope my life was a good example for you. I love each one of you. I pray you never loose faith in God. He is the only one who can help you.

I love you so much. It was you who kept me going. You stayed by my side through the good time and the bad time. We made it together. I always felt like I was your mother, then your big sister and last your best friend.

I know you all thought I was mean, but now, that you have children and have your husband and wife to help you with them, now you know why I had to be strict with you. God was on my side. I pray that God will always be at your side to help you to cope with life.

May God bless you and keep you in His care. I will always love you and keep you in my prayers.

Don't forget me when I am gone.

I love you,

MaMa"

THE RING

You are my inheritance, O Lord.
Psalm 16, 6.

**Audrey Enrica Boswell wearing MEA
on her First Communion Day 2011.
She is one of the children named after Mama.**

15

HISTORY OF THE RING

The ring has been named MEA (Maria-Enrica-Antici). It is a lovely piece of jewelry that has been in the family for at least 100 years. It belonged to Maria Antici and was probably purchased for her by Filippo Antici, my grandfather, in 1911 or 1912 when the couple went to Ostra, Italy, to help his father gather in the crop. We cannot imagine it being purchased elsewhere. According to two jewelers, the stone is probably a rough cut chip from a larger diamond that has never been polished. The mount is beautiful. It is gold, but has no marking as to carat. For that matter, it has no marking whatsoever which makes it unique. There were two rings, this engagement ring and a wedding band, both of which are wide to fit our five by five Grandma's finger.

119

After her death in 1981, Edith, Mama, Lena and Theresa drew straws for her jewelry. Mama got the engagement ring and she left it to me in her holographic Will. I gave the ring to my daughter, Celia St. Columbia, and the story of MEA begins with her.

In January 2010, we read the book *THE NECKLACE* about some women in California who purchased a diamond necklace and took turns enjoying it. We thought, why not the engagement ring. So, on February 20, 2010, Mildred, Vicky, Celia and I met Mary Ann and Susan at Davis-Kidd Book Store in Memphis. Excitement was in the air as we revealed the plan to share the ring with each other. We decided to keep it for one month and then pass it on to the next person, much like they do with the diamond necklace. Mildred being the oldest, got the ring first. Then Mary Ann and me. Our children have taken the ring places. She has been to Florida, Missouri, Tennessee, Texas, Illinois, Arkansas, Mississippi, Alabama, Georgia, and Nevada. We hope she will travel a lot more. She has attended mahjong games, Saturday night parties, baseball games, soccer games, birthday parties, was present for the birth of great, great grandson, Wilkes Bradham, my youngest grandchild, in August 2010, and Vicky had the ring in November 2011 when Bradley Rybolt welcomed his daughter, Grandma's great, great, great granddaughter, into the world.

MEA went on a biking trip to Boston in the fall, adding Massachusetts to the states she has traveled to.

In January 2012, she was off again to Las Vegas for a week of fun. MEA will be in two weddings this spring, one here in Clarksdale and one in Atlanta.

We have a journal for entries about what and where. We also encourage everyone to make pictures of themselves with MEA during their month. I happened to have MEA the night my two grandsons, Vance and Reed, played football in Arcola, Mississippi, where Grandma and Grandpa began their married life together in 1909.

The photo album has a wonderful picture of Grandma wearing MEA. There is a picture of Mama and Daddy on their wedding day. One of Mama when she was a beautiful young lady, one of us four kids when we were kids and one of the three girls with Mama when we were grown.

We also have pictures of those who have had the ring for one month showing off MEA at whatever event they have been to. Every time I get a chance to read the stories and look at the pictures, my heart just swells.

We hope the tradition of sharing the ring continues and expands to the next generation of descendants of Filippo and Maria Antici.

It's been almost 100 years since my grandparents began their married life here in America. Today, their descendants, numbering almost 200, are at home in many states across our great country.

THE FAREWELL

The Lord is with me to the end.
Lord, your love endures forever.
Psalm 138, 8.

16

GOODBYE, MGB

Mama loved that old avocado green Ford the grandchildren affectionately called the MGB (Mamaw's green bug). We almost had her convinced to buy a new car once, but she just couldn't part with the Ford. Even though the doors didn't always open, the windows didn't always roll down, or up, if you got them down, she loved it.

In the car, was a trash box, red, but you were not allowed to put trash in it. You kept your trash in your own pocket.

I'm not sure if the heater worked, but I am almost certain it did not have a working air conditioner, nor do I know with certainty that it even had air.

Because she lived in a curve, the car was hit a number of times and had been painted at least once, but she still loved it.

One day I was pulling into the Kroger parking lot and saw Mama's car in the lot. As I parked, I noticed that she was in the car and walked over to speak to her. I stupidly said, "Hey, what are you doing?" She was quick to tell me she was locked inside her own car. The one door that still opened from the inside would not budge. The windows would not roll down. Passersby merely waved at her when she waved at them – for help. How can you keep from laughing?

We thought surely she would sell the MGB, but still she just couldn't. With a rope tied to the door that would not let the door shut completely, she continued driving. And, yes, she held onto the other end of the rope. We found a door in a junk yard, and had the door fixed, painted yet another shade of green and she kept on driving. I think she liked that antique tag.

We sold the car for $200 after her death. It was the only item we sold. I just wonder if MGB is still running.

Mama, dear lady, you will always be loved and cherished in our memory.

ABOUT THE AUTHOR

I am so content with life. My husband and I live in Clarksdale on a quiet street with our two dogs. Cindy, the oldest, is the most loveable mutt on planet earth, and Angel, a shih tzu, is my teddy bear.

If you ring the doorbell and we don't answer, just walk around to the side of the house. Dub and I will probably be sitting on the patio enjoying our back yard. He is a knowledgeable gardener. I am just a lover of all growing things. We have an herb garden and a vegetable garden (much like my Grandma had) and enjoy fresh and fresh-frozen vegetables all year long.

The children live close by. Our greatest moments are when they are coming for a meal. How I savor those times. We start the day attending Mass together as a family and then eat, usually homemade spaghetti, and whatever else they think they might want.

We are faithful. Our blessings are many. The threads that bind us together are strong.

Additional copies of The American Dream
are available through your favorite
book dealer or from the publisher:

Bradham Press
346 Sandy Cove
Clarksdale, MS 38614-2317
Telephone: (662) 902-3064
E-mail: BradhamPress@yahoo.com

The American Dream
ISBN Softbound: 978-0-9858386-0-7, $18.95
Add $5.50 shipping for first copy
($2.00 each additional copy)
plus sales tax for MS orders.

To contact the author
Phone number: (662) 627-4630
E-mail: JoAnnKersh@yahoo.com

CPSIA information can be obtained at www.ICGtesting.com
Printed in the USA
LVOW042006161112

307421LV00002B/4/P